Econovation

Econovation

THE RED, WHITE, AND BLUE PILL FOR AROUSING INNOVATION

Steve Faktor

WILEY

John Wiley & Sons, Inc.

Published by John Wiley & Sons, Inc., Hoboken, New Jersey.
Published simultaneously in Canada.

For general information on our other products and services or for technical
support, please contact our Customer Care Department within the United States
at (800) 762-2974, outside the United States at (317) 572-3993 or
fax (317) 572-4002.

Wiley also publishes its books in a variety of electronic formats. Some content
that appears in print may not be available in electronic books. For more
information about Wiley products, visit our web site at www.wiley.com.

Library of Congress Cataloging-in-Publication Data:
Faktor, Steve, 1973-
  Econovation : the red, white, and blue pill for arousing innovation / Steve
Faktor.
       p. cm.
  Includes index.
     ISBN 978-1-118-05400-0 (hardback)
1. United States–Economic conditions–2009-   2. United States–Economic
policy–2009-   3. Technological innovations–Economic aspects–United
States.   I. Title.
  HC106.84.F35 2012
  658.4'063–dc23

                                                        2011037183

Printed in the United States of America

10 9 8 7 6 5 4 3 2 1

To my wonderful parents
for taking the ultimate risk to bring us to this amazing country;
at the age of six,
I was in no condition to escape the Soviet Union on my own!

Contents

Acknowledgments

My deepest gratitude goes to Deborah and Heyden for consuming every imperfect morsel of my early draft and giving me the kind of honest feedback and encouragement that could only come from true friends. Alex, you came along at exactly the right time to help me refocus on what really mattered, thank you, really. Yoav, I'm grateful for all your thoughtful advice and no, I'm not running for office, but the fact that you asked let me know I was on the right track. A special thanks to my friends Alison, Jon, Suparna, and Judith for inspiring me during this fun and challenging ride. Simran, I know I tortured you with lots of spreadsheets, but you did terrific work and I know you'll do amazing things in the future! To my editors Susan and Jennifer at John Wiley & Sons, I'm incredibly grateful to you for being so supportive of this project from the very beginning and for your kind patience as I did my best to juggle work, life, and writing deadlines.

What Is Econovation?

From the ashes of the Great Recession rises a great nation. That nation is China. How did this happen? Is the beacon for capitalism finally dimming? Is America destined to wallow in debt like Greece or some C-list celebrity? Or, will our legendary ingenuity save us from tweeting and eating our way to irrelevance? *Econovation* is a bold, witty response to those questions that doesn't rely on miracles or government for answers. It explores what the next decade of the U.S. economy will bring and the opportunities it will create. Think of *Econovation* as a trends book on steroids. It's bursting with practical, thought-provoking ideas no executive, entrepreneur, or Fed chairman can afford to miss.

In the past 30 years, the U.S. economy has ignited and extinguished more opportunities than any other force, with the possible exception of Oprah. In that time, China and India used their labor surpluses to feed the West's zombie-like appetite for iPhones, Prada, and Snuggies. That lifted millions out of poverty while their biggest customer, the United States, found itself in debt, undereducated, and covered with recreational tattoos. The situation feels unfamiliar, but clues to our future abound. The math points to another crisis or decade of tough, but cathartic choices to stave off irrelevance—or worse, the rise of a scarier, twitchier Coffee Party.

Today, it's become virtually impossible to see where government ends and business begins. The government is a huge buyer that can move markets or make rules that can sprout or kill industries. Low-income home loans, tax preparation, health insurance, farming, and several other industries mostly exist because of government. Others like energy trading, coal mining, marijuana (medicinal, of course), charter schools, cigarettes, liquor, and gambling are like veal—only allowed to grow to the size of the government's cage. Ironically, some of the most regulated industries now need innovation most. As public resources shrivel, economic policy and innovation will have to adapt.

I can't say that what policymakers have done so far is inspiring. If this were a game of Supermarket Sweep, where you have one minute to fill your cart with a year's worth of groceries, ours would be filled with Kit Kats, Twinkies, and Dr. Pepper. Short-term stimulus, health care reform, and cash for clunkers were loaded with empty calories. Not a single can of green beans in that cart. Without a major growth spurt, 70 percent tax rates, or big spending cuts, our $15 trillion debt could make U.S. dollars as useful as they are delicious. Speaking of dollars, we are still one of the only countries that can print its own money to trade for tangible goods, from oil to salami. That power opens a fleeting window of opportunity to create the next boom in efficiency-oriented technology, exports, and employment.

Employment is a recurring theme in *Econovation*. As with anything in life, it was only once jobs disappeared that people realized how much of their identity was based on them. Even those still employed felt a sudden emptiness. For a while, shopping and materialism defined them. But with the loans gone, everyone from executives to administrators suddenly hungered for meaning and purpose. As both people and country search for their next identity, *Econovation* offers tactical ways to reinvent consumerism and profitably rebuild the American identity.

This book is not a how-to book; it's a what-to. My goal is to help executives, entrepreneurs, and academics think differently about building sustainable innovations for the next decade. Using clues from our past, *Econovation* offers a new perspective on a future we've taken for granted. Even on a 12-step program, our economy can perform miracles that would have required an ark thousands of years ago. I'm not saying that innovation happens *because* of economics. I am saying that the success of what's invented will be determined by economic conditions. Anticipating those conditions can help businesses know where to look for opportunities, inefficiencies, and ideas.

By the time you're done reading *Econovation*, I hope it's well past the bookstore's return policy. More importantly, I expect you'll agree that opportunistic economics, the core of *Econovation*, should be wired into every business function—from strategy to product development to marketing. It can play a dominant role in the portfolio of trends that affect your business, consumers, employees, suppliers, and investors. I know this can be a heavy subject, so I did my best to put it on a diet. With a healthy mix of big ideas, data, and humor, I wouldn't be surprised if you bought a fresh copy of *Econovation* for every room in the house.

Why Me? Why Now?

Not long ago, I was a bleary-eyed student, trying to unravel the mysteries of some musty economics textbook. Those were innocent times. Books had all the answers. It took years for my swagger to turn into a limp when the recession hit. Economics turned out to be nothing more than a Pandora's box of human fear and frailty. The economy is an uncontrollable force dressed up in math, which makes you feel like you're in control when clearly you are not.

Though I have an economics degree from New York University, my career has been dedicated to creating and bringing innovations to market. Working with C-level executives at Fortune 500 companies, I've created multiple $100-million-plus businesses, deployed three enterprise-level innovation programs, and brought numerous products and services to market. My many creations (children?) live in stores and wallets worldwide. In recent years, I've also become a popular keynote speaker on the future of business and my 4Cs of Innovation™ methodology. I also muse poetically . . . and sometimes prophetically, about big ideas and ways to implement them at ideafaktory.com.

Yes, it was quite a ride . . . until 2008. For someone who makes a living from creativity, optimism, and building things that employ people, 2008 was a rude awakening. When the recession hit, a good chunk of my $50 million Chairman's Innovation Fund budget disappeared, as did a third of my personal savings. Entire industries buckled. Friends, colleagues, and countless others were left jobless. For the first time in my career, I had to lay people off and send them off into a cold, uncertain world. It was sobering. It felt like some cultish apocalypse, minus the Kool-Aid. I found myself on unfamiliar ground—fortunate to have a job, but with a little extra time on my hands. Instead of using that time to mourn losses in my portfolio, I became obsessed with trying to piece together what went wrong.

I tore through thousands of articles, historical examples, and expert predictions. It all became clear to me—I needed a more cheerful hobby! I was awed and humbled by the conspicuous piles of incompetence, shortsightedness, and outright criminality I found. Experts had no excuse not to see this coming or prevent something this preventable. Mostly, I was mad at myself for getting lulled into complacency given the sad state of global finance. Instead of wallowing in past mistakes or discovering medical marijuana, I decided to finally put a perfectly good economics degree to use. No challenge ever fazed me, so cracking the code on macroeconomics would be no exception.

In 2008, at the height of uncertainty, I put together a series of talks called "Recessionomics—A Path to Recovery." It was my chance to shine a light on what was happening in our economy and help others prepare for what might come next. These became so popular I ended up doing over a dozen sessions for hundreds of executives and staff across American Express. So many of them thanked me for helping soothe their incredible anxiety about what was happening. I was just happy when nobody cried! Their positivity was gratifying, but something was missing. People craved guidance—they wanted a way to apply Recessionomics to their personal and business lives. Though my prognosis wasn't full of rainbows and marshmallows, I had plenty of ideas. So I challenged myself to apply innovation principles to what was happening in the world. I wanted to translate turmoil into opportunity. I called this witches' brew Econovation™.

Since 2009, I have presented various flavors of Econovation at over half a dozen conferences. Attendees have consistently ranked me as a top keynote speaker. Maybe some of that was for my tasteful wardrobe and meticulous hygiene. More likely, it was for the deeply resonant subject matter. After every presentation, executives approached me with compliments, questions about the future, and invitations to speak at their companies. Some even asked me what career their son or daughter should pursue.

As Econovation evolved and I gathered insights and reactions from business leaders, I knew it was time to share my ideas in full bloom. So here we are. You hold in your hand the sum of three and a half years of my toil. It's an innovator's take on an economy gone wild and what to do about it—a melding of two very different worlds. This copy of *Econovation* might make me $1 richer, but I expect you'll gain far more . . . so feel free to include me in your will.

One More Thing

More than anything, I am a patriot. At the age of six, I immigrated to the United States from the Soviet Union. By the time my parents took that brave, fateful gamble, I'd already learned a lot of tough lessons. I learned the hard way that the *Pravda* newspaper was nowhere near as quilted as Charmin (I only wish that were a joke). I knew what it was like to wait in long lines for scarce resources dished out by unmotivated slugs. To my parents and their friends, the United States was a mythical land of endless possibilities, almost like Oz (think Emerald City, not the HBO prison show). America beckoned with hope, opportunity, and Cheetos. My parents left good jobs as a music teacher and an engineer to start from scratch in the most foreign of lands: Brooklyn, New York. Growing up wearing hand-me-downs and shopping for irregular underwear at the 99-cent store can be pretty humbling. It's not unlike what millions of Americans are experiencing now. I took it as a challenge to be that much smarter, more resourceful, and hard-working to make up the difference. That's the spirit in which this book is written. I feel a deep sense of obligation and gratitude to this tarnished but still great nation. If I contribute, even in a small way to its revival, I promise never to write anything this melodramatic ever again.

Don't get me wrong; I'm not mistaking this book for altruism or charity. To me, helping a business to grow, make products people want, and employ people is the ultimate sustainable charity. In turn, those employees can afford to send their kids to school, support their communities, and pay taxes. Trust me, we'll need every penny. And why do we still mint pennies?

The Next 100 Years

In terms of Econovation, it's hard to discuss the near future without at least considering the distant one. Clues to the next 100 years stretch from pyramids in Mexico to iPhones in Dubai. From the moment our furry ancestors discovered how to smash open coconuts with rocks, we haven't looked back. Every invention—shoes, the wheel, clocks, electricity, assembly lines, cars, and computers—made life on earth a little more bearable. Farmers in Vietnam can do more with a rake than their ancestors could with bare hands. The ones with tractors are on easy street. The spread of technology made it possible to sustain larger populations, trade globally, and communicate in ways that make the deck of the *Starship Enterprise* look like a finished basement from the 1970s.

In economic terms, we are part of a massive shift from labor to capital. Advanced countries like Germany build machines that run factories, seed crops, and transport energy. Others, like the United States, don't make much anymore. We left slaving over hot assembly lines to developing nations. Today, those with college degrees are hyperconnected cubicle dwellers. Their clicks, tweets, and "Likes" are shouts of a plump nation rejoicing in victory.

Like it or not, we are on a trajectory. Our future is digital. Power shifted to Droids, bloggers, and doughy MIT brainiacs faster than anyone could imagine. Just as in *Terminator, The Matrix,* or any self-respecting sci-fi dystopia, we are pulling away from the mundane limitations of the physical world toward the limitless possibilities of the digital one. In that future, machines make machines, not factories full of workers. Machines will grow genetically engineered, supercrops that feed billions. Those who have the skills will design, engineer, and program that future. They, and the companies they work for, will either build our digital realm or make our rare trips out of the house at least as enjoyable as Second Life on Xbox.

As everything hurdles toward automation, there can only be so many jobs dusting Donald Trump's garish furniture. That leaves one important question: What will the rest of the population do?

Employment wouldn't be as big a problem if the United States had managed its money at least as well as an entry-level accountant. The country that invented or perfected electricity, mass production, flight, cars, and the Internet should be filthy rich. Everyone in the U.S. should live like an oil sheikh—sitting on billions, looking for new investments and deciding which headdress to wear. Unfortunately, that's not how things turned out. Not only are we not rich, many people and our government are massively in debt. Adding insult to injury, we've surrendered our engines of growth, production, and employment to other countries in exchange for some cheap, lousy T-shirts. So now what?

The world's trajectory doesn't change. One way or another, we are all being drawn into *The Matrix*. I can't say I'm thrilled about it, but the United States, like other countries, must find its place in getting us there. The challenge we face is how to retool a large nation to make up for our financial missteps. Otherwise, we risk creating economic conditions that even our best innovators can't overcome. I know that sounds like government work, but that's what got us to the brink in the first place.

Coming Up in *Econovation*

In this flavor of *Econovation*, I focus on the world as it will be, not as it should be. That means offering businesses and individuals new ways to capitalize on the trajectory of this strange and disobedient economy. Here's a quick description of what you are getting yourself into, in the pages that follow:

Chapter 1—Indulgence in an Age of Constraint

Chapter 2—Tawdry Tales of a Service Economy

Chapter 3—The Next Decade

Chapter 4—Sell Actualization

Chapter 5—Build a Capital Magnet

Chapter 6—Make Makers

Chapter 7—Liberate Micropreneurs

Chapter 8—Build an "Incentive Nation"

Chapter 9—Unfinished Business

Appendix—Applying Econovation: How the Sausage Was Made

Looking at the flow of this book, I'm reminded of Charles Dickens' *A Christmas Carol.* Just think of the next chapter as a visit from the Ghosts of Economics Past and Present (played by me, though Jake Gyllenhaal almost got the part).

1

Indulgence in an Age of Constraint

Do you ever drive an air-conditioned sedan to your suburban home, stare at your flat screen and GE appliances and think, "Oh my God, I'm rich!"? Many Americans don't. A lot has to do with the bills that come at the end of each month. It's gotten hard to tell which things you own and which ones own you. In the last 30 years both the U.S. government and its citizens plunged into this raging sea of contradictions. Consider the following:

- If the United States is the wealthiest country in the world, why are we so deep in debt? Bernie Madoff could produce results like this.
- How can the stock market be soaring when unemployment is over 9 percent and few people trust stocks?
- We tout Twitter and Facebook as great inventions, but all the gadgets that make them possible are made overseas, occasionally by children.
- If the U.S. is so creative, why is our education system consistently ranked somewhere between Guam and Kazakhstan?
- Can a country this obese ever be competitive? It didn't work in gym class, why would it now?

From the public debate and rhetoric, you'd think we solved all the real problems. Politicians spend months squabbling over $90 million for National Public Radio when our deficits are in the trillions. They are either cynical opportunists or *thisclose* to wearing mother's wig in a desolate motel. We didn't suddenly wake up this way. Years of misguided policies, corporate greed, and individual complacency definitely helped.

Lots of books wallow in the seeds of America's decline. This is not one of them. I am more concerned with its resurrection. To do it, innovators will need some clues from our past. What follows is the story of our economic history as told by someone with no political affiliation and one too many pop-culture references.

The Way We Were

Many people blame capitalism, borrowing, and loose regulation for the economic collapse of the late 2000s. The truth is it's all of the above and then some.

Get Up, Stand Up (1900s)

The year 1900 marked a huge economic milestone. It's when the dollar became officially linked to gold. You might say a century is a long way to go to make a point, but like Charles Dickens, I get paid by the word. Actually, a country's reputation can take decades to establish and sometimes minutes to wreck. When the dollar's value was backed by gold, a lasting, sensuous love affair blossomed. Despite a few trysts with other currencies, everyone from French trendsetters to gruff Chilean miners accepted dollars.

A good example of how economic conditions connect to innovation can be found in a very peculiar place, the Great Depression. Nine out of 10 doomsayers agree—the 1930s were a worst-case scenario. At a time when stockbrokers jumped out of office buildings and horses pulled gasless cars, as you can see in Table 1.1, some enduring inventions thrived. Economic conditions played an important role in those successes, as they did during the dot-com boom of the late 1990s.

Throughout the industrial revolution, the United States was a sensible borrower. It used long-term debt to finance bridges, roads, and shiny new tanks to fight the original Axis of Evil. These investments almost always paid off in more commerce and taxes. While other Western nations removed shrapnel from landmarks, the U.S. economy bloomed. From the 1940s through the early 1970s,

Table 1.1   Depression-Era Innovations and the Role of Economics

Invention	Economic Theme	The Role of Economics
Supermarket	Scale, One-Stop Shop, Discounts	In a time when money was tight and gas was expensive, having a store with huge bargaining power that can provide one-stop shopping, eliminate multiple trips, and offer superior discounts is an economist's dream. It's also a template for the future.
Laundromat	Capital Pooling	Pooling of expensive capital that is used infrequently into a pay-per-use model has become common. Rental cars, arcades, and gyms are all modern incarnations of this model.
World's Fair	Tourism, Import Capital, Repurposing, Hope, Community	To create the Chicago World's Fair, unused land and garbage dumps were repurposed into a worldwide tourist attraction. Out of thin air, a magnet for tourism and foreign capital was created. The fair also gave people hope and a sense of community between two wars.
Monopoly	Escapism, Home-Based Entertainment	Monopoly was the epitome of cheap, affordable, home-based entertainment. When money to go out and travel was tight, extra leisure time could be spent ruling the world. Well, a fantasy world. This was a feel-good substitute for real success, which eluded many.
Miracle Whip	Substitution, Affordable Indulgence	Miracle Whip was more wallet-friendly and flavorful than the mayo it replaced. It added much-needed flavor to the cheaper, blander foods people were buying at the time. The fact that it's endured this long is a miracle of sorts. The fact that I still have a jar from 1999 in my fridge, even more so.
Sliced Bread	Efficiency, Convenience	Buying thin slices of sandwich bread was far more convenient and economical than making thick, irregular slices on your own. It was also a great portion control method that allowed people to budget by the slice.
Baseball All-Star Game, Superman, Bugs Bunny, Wizard of Oz, Marx Brothers	Hope, Escapism, Heroes, Charity	Economics is as much about psychology (consumer confidence) as it is about numbers (GDP). Hope has a powerful effect during times of hardship. From baseball all-stars to invincible fantasies like Superman, heroes are conduits for hope. Superman, Bugs Bunny, and the Wizard of Oz offered affordable escapism, like movies, video games, and the Internet do today. Entertainment has become one of the most resilient parts of the economy.

U.S. growth was driven by urbanization, education, and raging baby-making. (You don't get a baby boom without breaking a few mattress springs from pent-up post-war hormones.) This created a thriving middle class that produced and consumed in relative balance. President Lyndon B. Johnson helped create safety nets like Medicare and Medicaid. These were made possible by steady growth and top-tier tax rates of 70 percent or more. This warm, loving government was also able to smooth out slow periods through spending on public works or an occasional war. Economically, it was Gum Drop Mountains and Candy Cane Forests as far as the eye could see. . . .

Cracks in the candy cane started to show in the '70s. By then, the U.S. made less, consumed more, and craved foreign oil like a child craves, well, candy. Despite two crises, we deferred a trip to Gasaholics Anonymous and kept consuming. Recession, inflation, high unemployment, reckless bank deregulation, and disco all followed suit. Most relevant to us now, 1972 marked the end of the gold standard. Like when Superman gave up his powers to be with Lois Lane, the U.S. dollar became an ordinary piece of paper backed only by a big reputation.

Glory Days (1980–early 1990s)

In retrospect, the election of Ronald Reagan, a former actor, fore-shadowed America's permanent shift to services . . . and to some really bad television. Like *Knight Rider* or *Baywatch*, Reaganomics featured a charming lead character working with a thin premise. On the plus side, the economy boomed. Marginal tax rates dropped by 25 percent, household incomes rose by $4,000, and inflation dropped. At the same time, our debt tripled. After all, Communists weren't going to shoot themselves from space! That cost money. The growing debt problem was masked by high growth, low unemployment, and the country's last manufacturing boom. Savings rates plummeted for people and government alike.

The centerpiece of Reaganomics was supply-side economics. That meant giving tax benefits to high earners and businesses, whose prosperity would then "trickle down" to everyone else. It's not exactly how the world works. When poor people make more money, they spend most of it because they often operate at a deficit. The wealthy already save. When they make more, they save even more. Some of that goes into savings accounts or stocks, which can provide business, home, or car loans. More often, that money is placed in conservative investments like government debt. Ironically, lower taxes on the wealthy meant that the government would need to borrow more. And, the relationship between low taxes on the wealthy and job growth was like David Hasselhoff's relationship to his talking car—mostly fictional.

Ultimately, it's hard to tell if the 1980s boom was Reaganomics in action or just a natural economic recovery. Regardless, George Bush got stuck holding the bag. He took over a Hummer government on Ford Fiesta revenues. When recession hit, he had to raise taxes to cover fat budget gaps.

We Didn't Start the Fire (Mid 1990s–2000s)

Under Bill Clinton, the economy (and select interns) thrived. In the dot-com era, highballs, lavish parties, and ping-pong tables defined business, instead of boring old revenues, profits, and cash flows. Behind the champagne and dot-*com*araderie, the Clinton administration planted three magic beans that would later sprout into the Great Recession:

Bean #1: The 1999 revision to the Community Reinvestment Act. This forced Fannie Mae and Freddie Mac, two questionable public entities involved in buying private mortgages, to lower lending standards and give home loans to poor people. They called this "subprime" lending. That's like calling someone with an IQ of 70 a "subvaledictorian." Ill-informed borrowers flocked to eager financial institutions for unaffordable, adjustable-rate mortgages that carried a hidden risk of rate increases.

Bean #2: Clinton's push for free trade. On the surface, the North American Free Trade Agreement or NAFTA and over 200 free-trade deals made sense. Unfortunately, a country with high wages, and a big population had a lot to lose in this scenario. What would follow is a 15-year bleed of manufacturing jobs with little to take their place.

Bean #3: A ruinous deregulation of financial services led by Robert Rubin, Clinton's treasury secretary, set the stage for Wall Street cowboys to ride the United States like a bull, then skewer and grill it. By allowing commercial and investment banks to not only kiss but go all the way in Wall Street's bordello, a flurry of financially transmitted diseases (FTDs) would be unleashed.

Because of the boom, George W. Bush inherited a one-year budget surplus in 2000, the country's first since 1969. That didn't last long. As the economy was about to enter a post-dot-com and post-9/11 slide, President Bush and Federal Reserve Chairman Alan Greenspan took a series of steps to fight off the coming recession . . . and guarantee a much bigger one down the road.

The first of these steps was keeping rates artificially low. This cheap money motivated people to stop saving, pump money into stocks, and borrow rabidly. A massive real estate frenzy was born. At its peak, even New York City's homeless could sell their cardboard boxes for $350,000. At the same time, President Bush cut taxes for the wealthy and took on big expenses like two wars and drug benefits for seniors. The deficit yawned by $4 trillion. As if that wasn't enough, the administration passed the mockingly named "American Jobs Creation Act of 2004." It gave companies tax breaks to move jobs overseas. GE moved its aviation leasing operations to Ireland to qualify, saving hundreds of millions of dollars annually.

It wasn't just the government that was playing games with money. Under-regulated financial firms opened a mortgage casino and gamblers came in droves. For a decade, Americans saved less than 1 percent, compared to 30 percent for Chinese. Borrowers chased home prices up the price pole. Money was so abundant some bought investment homes, summer cottages, and doghouses with Moen faucets. Others piled on second mortgages to buy things to fill these new homes—all assuming house prices could keep going up 10 percent a year. Suddenly, something you bought *because you were rich* became something you bought *to become rich*. Financial companies were more than happy to oblige. After all, investors were eating up these packaged loans. Expecting these chopped up investments— collateralized debt obligations (CDOs)—would go bad, companies like Goldman Sachs wanted a way to bet against them. Insurers like AIG and others gladly took that bet. So the credit default swap (CDS) was spawned. Piles of them were sold to Goldman and others. Turns out, they badly misjudged the risk. The underlying loans were toxic, but complicit credit agencies kept giving them stellar ratings. Finally, these risky inventions of the computer era exploded like marshmallows in a microwave. Goldman Sachs vehemently denies using CDOs to bet against the very securities they were selling to clients, but the evidence has been unkind.

Running on Empty (2007+)

In 2007, malignant financial companies, not unlike Bernie Madoff, were caught taking bets they couldn't cover. Some crumbled. Others were deemed "too big to fail." These bloated zombies were rescued by TARP and other pricey government acronyms. Not that TARP (Troubled Asset Relief Program) was unsuccessful. It likely prevented more panic and breathed life into the lungs of TV pundits. Its biggest failure was not punishing gross offenders and deterring future naughtiness, or at least, removing the taxpayer petting zoo from the Goldman Sachs cafeteria.

As people realized their houses weren't worth what they owed, many stopped paying. By then, millions of people who had counted on home values for retirement, learned their nest egg contained a rotten little chicken. As lending dried up, the retail orgy that gripped the U.S. climaxed. Our one-trick, retail economy stood like the naked emperor, for all to gawk at. Hundreds of stores vanished.

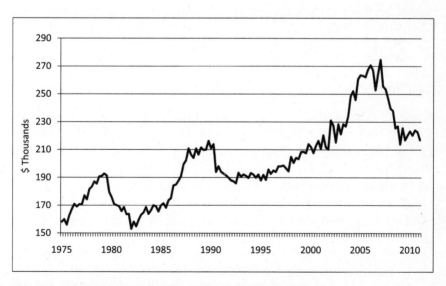

Figure 1.1   Median Single-Family Home Prices, 2010 (inflation adjusted)
Source: Bureau of Labor Statistics (BLS).

Industries like construction, auto, and realty instantly shriveled. Millions were left jobless, with few job prospects, surrounded by the cheap, plasticky remnants of a fictitious affluence.

Unlike during past recessions in the United States and Japan, neither people nor government saved anything for this rainy day. Luckily, the United States still had good credit, a charming disposition, and the mystical beard of Ben Bernanke, chairman of the Federal Reserve. The government borrowed more and blanketed the country with low rates, stimulus checks, and billions of freshly printed dollars. Unfortunately, stimulus is just a sugar high when most things are made overseas and money spent doesn't recirculate. Harvard economist Robert Barro estimates the real return on every $1 of government stimulus to be $0.80. Since we make so little here, most of the $0.80 value went abroad. Basically, we stimulated China. How do you say thank-you in Mandarin?

As the recession lingered, few foreign investors wanted long-term U.S. bonds at ridiculously low rates. Instead, the Fed, part of the U.S. government, bought bonds from the Treasury, part of the U.S. government, with cash it made from fairy dust. The bonds we did sell to investors were of the 3- to 10-year variety, not 30 years, like in the good old days. When you're borrowing to eat and not grow, a 30-year bet on your future is a lot to ask. Instead, China, Saudi Arabia, and others looked elsewhere for investments. China started buying up resources in Africa, reinvesting in infrastructure, and shutting down its "Made in the USA" label factories.

Right Now

Some check football scores to see how their fantasy teams performed. I check the World Economic Forum for country rankings. Fun at parties? You bet I am. In the 2010/11 report, the U.S. fell to fourth place in global competitiveness, but 87th place in the macroeconomic environment. Sure, Tajikistan had a good year, but what's our excuse? When you drill into the ratings, which are definitely more prestigious than *People*'s Sexiest Man Alive list, you'll find three things dragging everything down:

1. Balanced budget
2. Government debt
3. National savings rate

In those categories, we ranked near the bottom among 139 countries. (I don't recall who was dead last, but it would be safe to bet that its ruler has plenty of giant, heroic posters of himself.) Our fiscal problems are more serious than our cheerful number 4 ranking would indicate. Here's why.

Mesmerized by Debt

The debt spiral in Figure 1.2 applies to people and countries alike. Indebtedness explained in 15 simple steps:

1. It all starts innocently enough with wanting things. Sometimes, when you want things that are really expensive, like a mansion, a highway, or a missile defense system, you borrow.

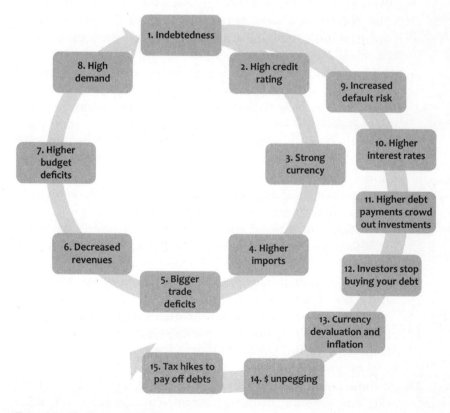

Figure 1.2   The Economic Spiral

2. If you make your payments on time, lenders love you. They express their love by sending love letters, also called "offers."

3. Word of your good credit travels far and wide. Others start offering you credit. After all, they know you'll pay the bills with a healthy interest. If you're a country, others feel comfortable buying your bonds and using your money.

4. Armed with lots of cash and a long shopping list, you borrow more. With the money, you can afford lots of expensive hobbies, like space travel, health care, and war. In fact, you can borrow so much, you barely have to work. You can pay other countries with lower wages to make you things. Or, you can bring in "guest workers" to do anything that requires movement.

5. Every year, you borrow just a little more than you earn. That's okay, you're still making payments.

6. If you're a country, your tax revenues start going down, since your citizens are now borrowing instead of producing. If you're an individual, there are fewer jobs because good credit has made others not work, either.

7. At some point, with enough people not working, the things you needed to buy, like bridge repair and health care are underfunded. Now you need to borrow more—this time, for necessities.

8. The cycle continues for a while, until the lenders start wondering if you'll ever work again. Or if your new job can produce enough income to pay your debts.

9. Lenders start thinking you're a higher default risk as you pace desperately through your hollow mansion.

10. They raise your rates. If you were just barely paying the interest before, just wait to see how hard it is to pay it with higher rates.

11. As more of your money goes toward paying debts, you can't afford the things to which you've grown accustomed—from wars to roads to that extra side of guacamole at Chipotle.

12. If things get bad enough, investors stop lending you money. In the case of the U.S., that's usually private companies and foreign governments.

13. At some point, you can either renegotiate your debts or inflate your currency by "printing" more of it. People can't make money, but the U.S. can. Either way, the value of your money

drops. In the inflation scenario, you still pay off your debt in nominal terms (the numbers are the same, but the value of each dollar is diminished). If you renegotiate, you pay a percentage on the dollar. Either way, your credit rating takes a hit, and you have to start rebuilding your credit score.

14. When your currency is worth less (or worthless), others stop using it and find alternatives, like other countries' money, precious metals, or wampum.

15. Once you've renegotiated, you really have to pay every cent. There are no second chances. The best way to do it is increase revenues. For a country that's higher taxes. For individuals, it's saving or a better paying job.

Bills, Bills, Bills

If you look at annual expenses compared to federal tax revenues in Figure 1.3, you'll notice one thing—things don't look good. Annual interest payments alone, threaten to eat us alive. On top of that, we have massive, growing obligations for Medicare, Medicaid, and Social Security. By 2040, our creditors will have jumped ship and we'll probably need to know Mandarin to vacation in Hawaii.

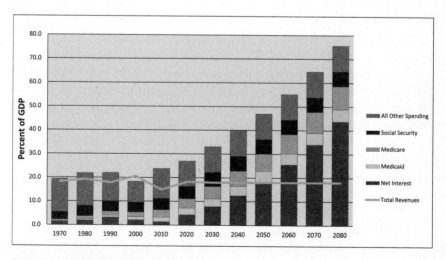

Figure 1.3   U.S. Debt Trajectory, 1970–2080

Source: Congressional Budget Office (CBO).

To get a sense exactly how massive the numbers in Figures 1.3 and 1.4 are, let's convert these exact proportions into a personal home loan for Sally Smith. Sally is 35 years old and earns $50,000 a year as a health care administrator. She wants to buy the house across the street from George Clooney. She is a big fan and thinks she found a bargain. To buy it, she needs to borrow just under $316,000. She plans to save an aggressive 25 percent of her income to pay off the loan. Sally's income is growing at 3 percent a year and her loan has a 6 percent rate. After 30 years, Sally will be earning $121,363 but will still owe more than $1.2 million. The loan was more than she could handle. By then, George Clooney is far too old and still indifferent to Sally's flirtations. Yet her debt remains. The only way Sally could have paid off the loan in 30 years was to save 40 percent of her income, not 25 percent.

The United States doesn't need to pay off its entire balance, but it needs to get to a point where that principal is going down, not up. There are three basic ways this can happen:

1. **Increase revenues** through higher taxes.
2. **Lower expenses** by cutting entitlements, military, and other major expenditures.
3. **Grow**. For example, if our friend Sally Smith found a more lucrative career in software development, she could double her income. In that case, the 25 percent she committed to saving would be more than enough to pay for her loan, if not attract the elusive Mr. Clooney, that silver-haired fox.

It's not an all or nothing situation. The final answer will need to be a mix of all three. As for the third, creating growth is by far the hardest. And, the role of government hasn't always been clear. In this incarnation of *Econovation*, I won't talk about what government can do to help Sally earn more. Instead, I'll focus on what Sally can do to help herself. If 30 million Sallys can't figure out how to improve their incomes, start businesses, and employ others, risks for the U.S. include:

1. **Crowding out.** This is the biggest risk if the United States doesn't change its trajectory. Remember, Sally planned to save 25 percent of her income to pay her debt. Imagine if her medical expenses were also growing at 20 percent a year.

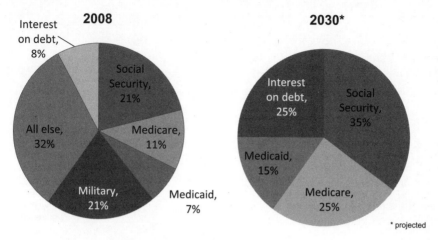

Figure 1.4   U.S. Expenses 2008–2030
Source: Congressional Budget Office (CBO).

Eventually, she'd only have debt and health expenses. That is what could happen to the United States by 2030. All we'll be able to afford are entitlements. See Figure 1.4.

2. **Interest rate hikes.** As the United States takes on more debt without increasing revenues, investors will start to doubt if U.S. debt is worth the risk. That will raise interest rates and reduce funds available for other programs. Or it could speed up inflation.

3. **Run on the banks.** Because so much of the U.S. debt is now short term, the government is rolling over (like expiring CDs) trillions each year into new bonds. Imagine some or many of these borrowers demanding their principal back, treating our bonds like shares of pets.com. They could flood the market with cheap U.S. bonds, sending the dollar into the dog house.

4. **Devaluation.** If the dollar sinks compared to other currencies or against hard assets like gold, oil, or ketchup, everything can get expensive—fast. This happened in Argentina during its financial crisis from 1999 to 2002. The government cashed out peoples' stocks, bonds, and foreign currencies to pay their debts. The Argentinean peso, which was worth $1.00, was cut down to a quarter of its value. Suddenly everyone was 75 percent poorer and 450 percent angrier. So you think that can't happen here? It already did. During the Great Depression,

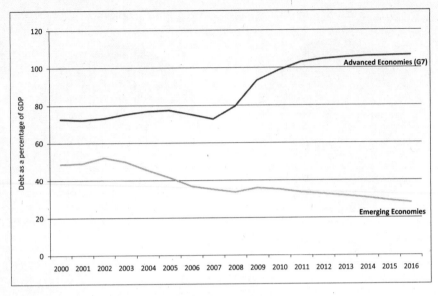

Figure 1.5   General Government Gross Debt Ratios, 2000 to 2016

Source: International Monetary Fund (IMF) World Economic Report, April 2011.

Table 1.2   The Way We Were (Summary)

1900s	1980–Early 1990s	Mid 1990s–2000s	2007+
Get Up, Stand Up	Glory Days	We Didn't Start the Fire	Running on Empty
1. Hello and good-bye gold standard 2. Industrialization and innovation 3. Borrow to build 4. Shift from manufacturing to services 5. Gas addiction	6. Reaganomics 7. Growing trade gap 8. Appreciating $ 9. Recession and first Iraq war/ oil crisis 10. Cheap is good	11. Deregulation 12. Low lending standards, liars and sharks 13. Tax cuts 14. Artificially low rates 15. "War on terror" 16. Increasing debt and budget deficits 17. Fake assets/CDS/ CDO 18. NAFTA kicks in: Jobs are for foreigners 19. Why save?	20. Bailouts 21. No penalties 22. For the love of debt 23. Printing money 24. Unemployment

President Roosevelt made owning anything but a tiny thimble-ful of gold illegal. People were forced to convert to dollars or face a $10,000 fine.

5. **Competitors win.** High-growth emerging markets are filling their piggy banks (see Figure 1.5). They don't borrow nearly as much and will have cash, good credit, and income growth that allows them to invest in infrastructure and education—in ways indebted Western nations can't.

So What?

After reading this chapter, you're probably thinking I'm never getting that job at Hallmark. Maybe so. Regardless, coming to terms with your past helps you move on. If that past is a sordid one, it also keeps you vigilant. It's that hyperawareness that will help businesses find opportunity. As we embark on that search, feel free to tear out Table 1.2 as a wallet-size reminder of where we've been. In Chapter 2, we'll go deeper into the major structural and demographic challenges U.S. innovators will face.

2

Tawdry Tales of a Service Economy

C oming out of the Great Recession, the United States, like a long retired boxer, finds itself with an odd-looking mix of muscle and flab. If innovation is how the United States plans to compete with China, India, and Brazil, it can't hurt to know what we'll have to work with. Sure, the other guys have massive factories, cheap labor, and exceedingly friendly phone support. Don't we have something even better—creativity, freedom, and "American spirit"? Shouldn't that close the deficit right up?

Botox and Other Services

Stripped of pricey homes, bustling malls, and material delights, the United States didn't look very sexy in its birthday suit. In the stillness of this new America, I began to notice something. No one I knew made anything. One possible exception was my recently retired dad. He was a hardworking, Soviet-trained engineer who designed custom storage containers at one of the last factories in Brooklyn. Surely, this wasn't the norm? It was. In the 1940s, 80 percent of the U.S. economy was based on production and manufacturing. By 2007, the equation flipped to 70 percent consumption and services. In 60 years, we went from pioneering carmakers to social media experts and Circuit City clerks. Starting in the late 1960s we also began generating massive trade deficits—from $400 billion to $700 billion a year. We want our iPads and Chilean sea bass, but we've been sending paper promises in return.

We call this new reality a "service economy." At the high end of the wage scale, services can include intellectual property (IP), like making *Avatar*, Windows 7, or Viagra. At the lower end, there's cleaning, cooking, and maintaining. Many in the middle, like legal, research, financial analysis, and customer support have already been shipped to India. The ones still here, from teaching to policing to nursing, are perfectly noble professions with one big challenge: Their work is not exportable.

If China sent 10 cases of Transformers toys to the United States, the dollars you paid for them are a promise that at some point, they can be redeemed for equal value. What if you didn't make anything they wanted? Faith in your money falters and its value falls. A pile of worthless green papers is of little consolation as you joyfully change your truck into a robot and back again. Long gone are the days when the dollar was backed by gold and the U.S. was an industrial giant. Still, the elite status of our currency stuck. That gave the country decades of goodwill. As we Tweet in the shadow of our former selves, our trading partners are getting sunstroke waiting at the dock for those ships filled with American goods to arrive.

Speaking of sunshine, without enough high income jobs, the U.S. starts to look a lot more like Jamaica than Singapore, two very different service economies with one thing in common—small populations. Jamaica has great land, beaches, and Ziggy Marley to attract tourists. Serving the needs of affluent globetrotters creates many of the country's jobs. This affords Jamaicans good but modest livings. That means no 401(k) plans, Botox treatments, or wasabi-encrusted filet mignons. Then there's Singapore, Asia's financial services hub. Its educated, global work force could swim in Botox, if it wanted. Because Singapore's services bring in foreign capital, it can import the rest without worrying about trade deficits or skimping on the wasabi. Like any economy, Singapore also has a lower paying service ecosystem of restaurants, bars, and shops. Most of the U.S. jobs created since the 1990s have been of this low end, gritty variety. In fact, except for government, education, and health care, all industries lost jobs from 1999 through 2009 (see Figure 2.1). As low earners service a globetrotting elite, the United States has the sleek styling of Singapore, but the economic engine of Jamaica.

Sailing Our Brand-New Entrepreneur Ship

We're not Jamaica just yet. And, we have a few years before the Chinese demand their Transformers back. When they do, will we

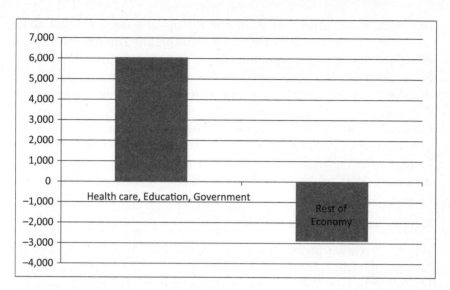

Figure 2.1   Changes in Jobs over Past 10 Years
Source: Bureau of Labor Statistics (BLS).

have new solar panels to trade for their piles of dollars? Will we sell them wind turbines? Plane engines? Or high-tech computer systems? It doesn't seem likely. Ambition still flows through America's arteries, but it might not produce something our trading partners want. Deep inside this new American dream beats a digital heart.

There's something incredibly liberating about living in a time when all you need is a computer and broadband to start a company that could someday be worth billions. As tech luminary Leo LaPorte points out, Mark Zuckerberg didn't have to ask AOL or CBS for permission to start Facebook. Nor did he have to endure the indignity of endless meetings and PowerPoint presentations. He just went out and did it . . . more accurately, he stayed in and did it. The United States is bursting at the seams with private investors waiting to heap cash on any company that has "social," "digital," "mobile," and "location-based" in its description. Small, traditional (analog?) businesses may not attract the same feeding frenzy, but they still have access to loans, affordable supplies, and an abundant workforce. They also benefit from good roads, law enforcement, and broadband infrastructure.

A recent example of our new, digital brand of innovation is the growth of virtual goods, which is expected to reach $5 billion in a few years. Companies like Zynga, Playfish, and Linden Labs make addictive games that have their own economies. You can buy magic swords to slay demons or digital roses to woo your pixilated princess. For a few dollars, everyone from stay-at-home moms to pale-faced dungeon masters can fling angry birds or rule a vast kingdom. In this economy, you don't need to build the sword factory, ship the roses, or make sure the magic potion has spill-proof packaging. These companies have innovated, but created very little halo effect of high earning jobs. Of course, you could always open a Subway sandwich shop across from Zynga's offices.

Creativity Isn't Reserved for Americans

When a creative problem comes up, Koreans don't beam a giant McDonald's logo into the sky to summon a portly American crusader to solve it. In fact, while George W. Bush restricted stem cell research, South Korea developed the technology to clone an entirely new George W. Bush. Their advances were made possible by government funding.

According to an IBM poll of 1,500 CEOs, creativity was considered the number one leadership competency. Yet the Torrance test, a respected global creativity exam, shows U.S. scores have been declining since 1990. Ironically, American education has reversed course with China and the rest of the world. While we've become obsessed with standardized tests and memorization, European and Chinese schools are adopting problem-solving curricula. Some Chinese schoolboys are figuring out how to build a moped while American kids are struggling to name the capital of Wisconsin.

China will not settle for the $100 Sharper Image gift certificate in science. As the West slashes budgets, China's spending on R&D has tripled in the last 15 years. By 2020, it will be 2.5 percent of the country's GDP—about the same as the United States. In 2011, China announced a $23 million plan to lure science superstars (Nobel Prize winners, professors, and the guy who invented Chicken and Waffles) to its shores. The United States did the same with Albert Einstein and others during World War II. It remains to be seen how the lure of cash compares to fear of persecution as motivator. The U.S. still leads the world in scientific publications and citations, but its share has dropped to 21 percent. From 1993 to 2008, China's share has more than doubled to 10.2 percent with similar surges

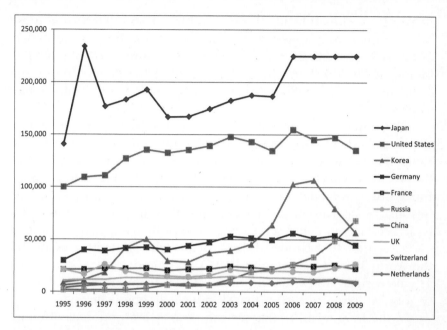

Figure 2.2   Patents Granted by Country of Origin of Applicant
Source: World Intellectual Property Organization (WIPO).

from Brazil, India, South Korea, and Turkey. Still, things are far from perfect in China. Scientific competition and plagiarism run rampant, and many scientists leave the country once they get a taste of the opportunities and delicious pastries found abroad. See Figure 2.2.

What does all this mean for the future of U.S. innovation? We still have a great team, but our players are aging and competitors are getting better coaching. The risks of placing all our bets on the "knowledge economy" are starting to show. Others are on the verge of creative parity and have the means to build their creations. Brains and beauty is a deadly combination.

Ideas Are Export-Challenged

We might not corner the market on great ideas, but the U.S. has many companies creating great intellectual property in software, pharmaceuticals, and entertainment. These idea-based products are much harder to export—or too easy to get for free. Many emerging markets have a hard time respecting ideas. They love pirated copies of Windows, cloned U.S. web sites, and free Robert DeNiro movies. (Their popcorn, however, is not pirated.) According to the Office of the U.S. Trade Representative, the U.S. economy lost about $250 billion in 2005 due to piracy. The Institute for Policy Innovation estimates the United States loses a very precise 373,375 jobs a year to piracy.

There has been some progress in getting better IP protection and enforcement, but it's like getting your son excited for a root canal. The challenge is that piracy creates local jobs. Why license Yahoo! mail when a local company can copy it? For a long time, India only protected the process of producing a drug, not the formula. So if you stirred counterclockwise to produce the same basic Prozac, you could sell Fauxzac without paying a royalty to the patent owner. To compound the problem, the United States joined the World Trade Organization (WTO) to help defend its IP abroad. The downside? WTO rules prohibit the U.S. from protecting domestic jobs by taxing countries that dump cheap goods here.

In the long term, IP patents can destroy innovation as often as they create it. As Google's Senior Vice President and General Counsel Kent Walker points out, "A patent isn't innovation. It's the right to block someone else from innovating." That blockage creates jobs for lawyers, not innovators. Maybe the U.S. respects IP *too much*. By allowing protections for things like one-click checkout (Amazon), web page scrolling gestures (Apple), and the page up and down keys (Microsoft), the system gets clogged. Countless calories are burned moving sideways, defending marginal ideas, instead of making them better. Unfortunately, the United States can't afford to live in a world with no IP protection. It might spur more innovation, but when all you have to offer is ideas, you fight dearly to protect them.

Like a failed marriage proposal between innings at a World Series game, our lack of export leverage can get uncomfortable to watch. In 2010, U.S. executives and politicians meekly implored China to let U.S companies compete there, like Chinese firms do here. There was little incentive for them to go along. Many of our financial, software, and web services are already available across Asia—from China Union Pay credit cards to Alibaba, China's version of eBay. Facebook "likes" are hard to trade for freshly built hard drives.

When I sold electronics during college I learned to sell what's in stock, not what's in next week's shipment. I probably wouldn't have closed many sales if each of my customers also owned their own electronics stores. The U.S. has the same problem. By comparison, Germany never had to beg. Though it's much smaller, Deutschland still manufactures high-end goods, cars, and machinery. As the recession subsided, industry in Germany boomed. Mercedes and BMWs practically drove themselves to China—in bulk and on schedule.

The good news is that it's mostly upside from here. By now, much of what could be outsourced has been. Now we can start with a fresh perspective on things our trading partners want and can't make themselves. These can't be one-off events. The U.S. needs a domestic jobs defense strategy, just like it has for the military but without all the saluting and horns. Until that happens, companies can ride a cheaper dollar and government desperation to the Promised Land . . . in this case, the shores of Asia. More details to come in the Capital Magnet chapter.

Without Production, the Innovation Engine Stalls

Grassroots industrial innovation began in the early 1900s when assembly-line workers formed informal quality circles. They'd ask simple questions like, "Why do the parts always come in after 4:00 P.M., not at 5:00 A.M.?" "Why do the fenders have to come back through the factory to get painted?" Or, "Why is Lucy eating all the chocolates?" Seeing the problem led to solving it. Real, employee-driven innovation was born.

From 1979 through 2010, the United States lost 8.1 million manufacturing jobs, most of them in the past 10 years. When the Clinton administration eliminated trade barriers, we were flooded with cheap Nirvana T-shirts and cheerful call center support, but at what cost? This turned out to be a scorched earth policy. After the U.S. lost tens of billions of dollars in manufacturing wages, even the cheapest goods started to run out of customers. Now, with less than 11 percent of our economy in manufacturing, opportunities to innovate start to narrow. See Figure 2.3.

As Andy Grove, former CEO of Intel, recently wrote, "Not only did we lose an untold number of jobs, we broke the chain of experience that is so important in technological evolution . . . abandoning today's 'commodity' manufacturing can lock you out of tomorrow's emerging industry." Without R&D facilities, factory floors, and an ecosystem of suppliers, you lose the ability to tinker, refine, and

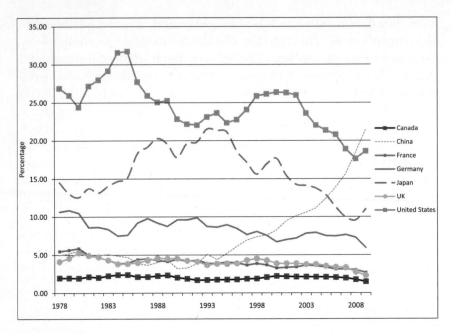

Figure 2.3   Shares of World Manufacturing
Source: United Nations.

reinvent. When the United States stopped making consumer electronics 30 years ago, it also stopped making batteries. When the market for laptop and car batteries heated up, our ability to compete was gone. Boeing and Gulfstream might be on that same path. Both make planes in the U.S., but many of the components are built elsewhere.

Their ecosystems are also slipping away. At best, they'll leave behind a repressed, needy form of innovation. It's like a relationship where one partner earns all the money and has all the power. Long after your beautiful courtship, guess who decides when it's time for dinner or sex? We are in that courtship phase. The carriage rides in the park are romantic, the electronic gifts, flattering. Still, precious knowledge and leverage drains from our well. If we don't change our path, not only will the next generation of inventions come from those who make them, we'll be having sex on their schedule, not ours.

There are companies trying to manufacture and create jobs in the United States, but the math doesn't quite work. Bill Watkins, who runs Bridgelux, wanted to open a factory in California to make electronic lights for office buildings and street lamps. He needed a few big contracts so he could produce at scale and compete on price. The factory would create hundreds of jobs, but he couldn't find U.S. customers with infrastructure budgets. Instead, he won contracts in China, India, and Malaysia. They greeted him with tax breaks, 10-year worker subsidies, and a lifetime supply of fish-based snacks. Abroad, Bill Watkins found growing, vibrant ecosystems starved for better infrastructure. Not only did the United States miss out on creating new jobs, but it was another pipe to the kneecaps of future innovation.

The Good Jobs Don't Scale

Losing lots of manufacturing jobs wouldn't matter if high-wage services could make up the difference . . . except the high end doesn't scale. There's a lot more work in making things than inventing them. Apple has about 25,000 employees in the United States, mostly in marketing, design, management, customer support, administration, and retail. By comparison, FoxConn has 250,000 employees making Apple products in China. That doesn't include jobs at suppliers like Samsung or Toshiba. Dell and Seagate Technology have similar 10 to 1 ratios.

Facebook, considered one of the most innovative companies in the U.S., is worth almost $90 billion but employs only 2,000 people worldwide. That's the population of my apartment building. Combined, top earning service industries (software, pharmaceuticals, financial services, engineering, and medical research) employ less than a million people in the United States. They're also not growing fast enough to replace the eight million jobs lost during the recession. That's like creating 320 companies the size of Apple. As for the 44 million people on food stamps, finding a low-skill job with decent pay is like finding a unicorn that also plays piano.

As Figure 2.4 shows, the Great Recession exposed just how few unicorns there were and how many people were chasing them. Much of this is structural, because jobs lost in the housing bubble—finance, construction, and real estate—are not coming back.

Haves versus Have-Nots

If you're lucky enough to have a white-collar job, you live in a time like no other. Food is plentiful, if genetically unsettling. Entertainment

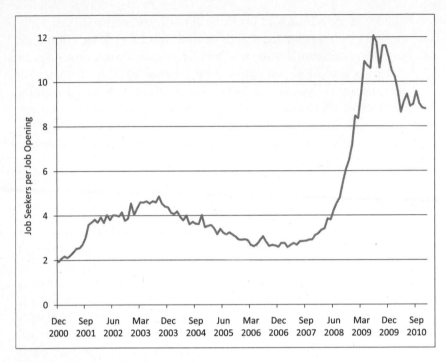

Figure 2.4   Ratio of Job Seekers to Job Openings

Source: Federal Reserve Economic Data.

waits at every turn. Are there any flat surfaces left without a touch-screen harboring some dreadfully addictive app? Everyone on the planet is instantly reachable. You can start a company without land or people. In fact, if you know how to program, you can make land and people—and magic spells that sell as if they were real. This is a renaissance of leisure. As I take a well-earned break from tweeting to actually work on something productive—this book—I don't need to look far for evidence of leisure and self-indulgence.

For the longest time, even those without high school diplomas benefited from the trickle down. Sure, their houses didn't have fountains and their coffee beans weren't picked by a mythical Colombian perfectionist, but they had abundance. As entire industries disappeared, their trickle turned into a stubborn drip. The Xbox proved a poor substitute for an education; the big house, an impossible burden without job prospects.

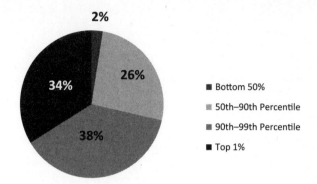

Figure 2.5   Distribution of U.S. Wealth, 2007

Source: State of Working America 2007, EPI.

Wealth Gap

Consider the distribution of wealth shown in Figure 2.5.

When the top 1 percent controls 34 percent of the wealth and the bottom 50 percent has only 2 percent, an important question comes to mind—will every figure in this book be depressing? No, it won't. The real question is: What is a sustainable way to put that 50 percent to work? There are midtier jobs that cater to the upper crust—retail, entertainment, tax preparation, and so on. Still, it's not enough. As wealth gets more concentrated, the halo of good jobs narrows. Can innovation make up the difference? I say yes. But the United States needs big ideas and flawless execution. To get there, we'll need a level of collaboration between government and business not seen since . . . since *now* in China. I'm not suggesting central planning or having your grade-schooler suit up for a 14-hour day at the Prada knock-off factory. I do mean a distinctly American flavor of collaboration that liberates that pent-up productivity buried deep inside our cheesecakes.

Income Gap

Now consider the distribution of income shown in Figure 2.6.

In 1965, the CEO of a Fortune 500 made 24 times an average worker's salary. Now, it's 344 times that—just enough to never have to grapple with the *venti* versus *grande* decision at Starbucks. Thirty years of bubbles masked the fact that income for 90 percent of

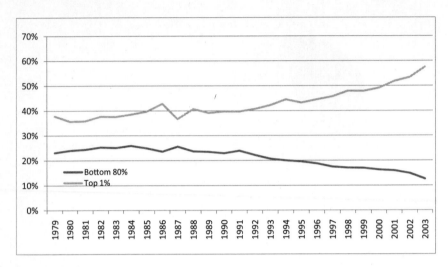

Figure 2.6   Shares of Capital Income, Top 1 Percent and Bottom 80 Percent, 1979–2003
Source: CBO.

Americans only grew by $280 a year. Their struggle to afford both futons and Vuittons became very real as the credit bubble burst.

Why Innovators Should Care about the Class Divide

If you paid over $20 for this book (or borrowed it from a wealthy friend), you might think these are not your problems. After all, you have a good job, clearly enjoy great literature, and nobody with food stamps can get within miles of your favorite Whole Foods. You are not as insulated as you think. There are some very real risks of creating two wildly separate classes of citizens.

Fewer Customers   The most basic challenge of a class divide is that people with impaired incomes can't buy your products. You can sell to the rich, but there's a limit to how much food, clothing, or shelter they can consume. From Oreos to laptops, a more balanced income distribution creates customers.

Vestment   An unbelievable 47 percent of households pay no federal taxes at all and only 46 percent of eligible people vote. A mere 35 percent of the unemployed vote. Almost half the population has little to no stake in this society. It's the difference between how you treat your own car and a rental: "Hmmm . . . I wonder what would happen if I put diesel in this thing?" Or, "What if I hit the brakes, clutch, and gas at the same time?" Over time, a car—or a country— wears down from the neglect.

Concentration Risk   Investors don't put all their money in one company; they diversify. The same concentration risk applies to relying on just a handful of customers. Over time, those customers gain enough bargaining power to squeeze margins and control your destiny. The United States has the same problem. The top 5 percent of the population makes most of the money and uses its disproportionate bargaining power to get lower taxes and other concessions from government. If 95 percent are economically impaired and the top 5 percent perpetually get lower taxes, how does the government run and repay its debts? Moreover, the top 5 percent has the economic mobility to leave.

Inflation, Scarcity, and the Revolt of the Underclass   For years, the U.S. did a fine job of pacifying even the marginally employed with Nintendo Wii's and salty, delicious fries. The calorically challenged do not look like revolutionaries, but years of unemployment and class separation can take a toll. With rising global demand for food, energy, and other resources, the wealthy can absorb price hikes. The unemployed and underemployed cannot. Extended bouts of underemployment can strain public benefits, increase crime, and degrade quality of life. As long as we are still knee-deep in Oreos, revolution is unlikely. As those cookie packages shrink and decent lower-skill jobs fade, don't be surprised to find the runners-up from *The Biggest Loser* pillaging your favorite Whole Foods.

Replacing High Earners with Low Earners   Simply put, rich people are not procreating; poor people are. As immigrants, my parents didn't need a supercomputer (at the time, a Commodore 64) to figure out that adding another child to our one-bedroom apartment would break the bank . . . or kill the romance. So, I remained an only child and got all my necessities at the 99-cent store. Today, it looks like that store is going to get a lot more customers. Consider California. It's one-seventh of the U.S. economy and offers a glimpse into our future.

According to the Public Policy Institute of California, the state's white population is on average, 44 years old, college educated, and has fewer than two kids per household. At an average of 28 years of age, Hispanics are much younger and have about three children per household or 3.7 for new immigrants. At just over $22,000 per year, they earn half of what white Californians earn, with one-tenth the net worth. That wouldn't be a problem if the U.S. was swigging Cristal on P. Diddy's yacht. The reality is, those who can afford the rising cost of education and health care aren't feeling frisky. Over time, that shrinks the tax base, strains public services, and packs the 99-cent stores.

Fossils and Fledglings

At polar ends of the demographic spectrum, two groups are on a collision course. The young hunger for jobs with decent pay, while those retiring expect big benefits from a shrinking, aging workforce.

When I'm 64

Western nations are getting old. Unless they rediscover the joys of sex and parenthood, countries like France, Germany, and the United States will all be eating at 5:00 P.M., in bed by 8:00 P.M., and complaining about all the noise. What noise? The champagne-soaked parties in China, India, and Brazil will go all night. Today, that noise comes from factories churning 14 to 16 hours a day in the hopes of someday becoming . . . us. (Or, U.S.) Figure 2.7 shows the colossal shift in population as birth rates in the East dwarf those in the West.

Just as high-paying jobs disappear, a flood of baby boomers will be retiring. And, they'll live longer than ever. In 1960, there were five workers paying taxes for each retiree. Soon, it will be half that. In 1960, life expectancy was just under 70 years. Today, it's approaching 80. With rising health care costs, fewer workers can afford longer retirements on lower incomes. Entitlements like Medicare, Medicaid, and Social Security will crumble under the weight of 10,000 baby boomers retiring each day. See Figure 2.8.

Something needs to change. But what politician is brave enough to stand up to these roving gangs of scooter-riding, cane-wielding

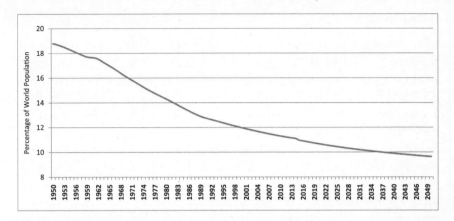

Figure 2.7   Population of the West as a Percentage of World Population
Source: United Nations.

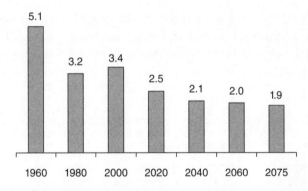

Figure 2.8   Number of Workers per Retiree

terrors? Sure, you could sabotage their walkers or lock them out of the country next time they vacation in Mexico, but change is inevitable. It'll either be done to us or by us. Japan and many parts of Europe find themselves in a similar place. At an average age of 42, Japan has one of the oldest populations, but their high savings rate gives retirees a buffer most Americans don't have. Lower savings and fewer benefits means old people will live longer, work longer, and possibly clog the pipes of opportunity for younger workers. Sixty-five-year-old skateboarders? Octogenarian outfielders? Forty-year-old interns? Anything is possible.

Forever Young

After World War II, workers with high school degrees could find high-paying industrial jobs with decent benefits. Back then, children could support their parents with nothing fancier than canned meat products and a massive, wooden radio for listening to Orson Welles. Today, parents spend 10 percent of their annual income supporting their adult children. According to a study by Princeton and the Brookings Institute, about 40 percent of kids move back in with their parents some time during their 20s. It's not because they miss Mom's meatloaf. In 1960, 77 percent of women and 65 percent of men completed the five milestones by age 30: finishing school, leaving home, becoming financially independent, marrying, and having a child. Today, many don't even chase those goals. Call it selfishness or independence, the results are the same: lower birth rates, higher personal expectations, and fewer ways to achieve them. See Figure 2.9.

By early 2011, college grads had an unemployment rate under 5 percent, compared to 9.5 percent for those who only made it through high school or 13.7 percent of those who dropped out. On the surface, college still seems like the surest path to a great job and

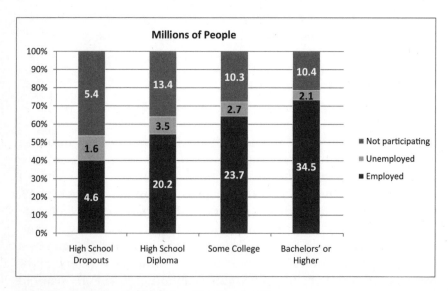

Figure 2.9   March 2011 Employment vs. Education, Age 25+

a bachelor pad with a stain-resistant couch. Once they get a job, college grads do earn more. But a crazy thing happened on the way to the frat house—the price of college got out of hand. Consider the following:

- An education that once gave you an $800,000 advantage in lifetime earnings now only offers a $280,000 edge. For many professions, there is no advantage. The spitball king of home-room can easily make more as a welder than the bookworm turned blogger. So many students burn lots of calories on education just to stand still.
- Salaries for college-educated workers haven't budged since 2000. Men average $72,000 a year and women, $52,000.
- New graduates under 25 have about the same unemployment rate as the overall population. The jobs don't seem to care if you have a degree or not. A diploma tucked in your drawer is of no consolation when your carpenter buddy from high school buys a new house, while you pay off a mortgage to IOUniversity.

The good news is college grads have a tendency to adapt to new technologies and industries as they pop up. If you can SMS, LOL, and OMG, you can probably become some sort of knowledge worker. For companies, this means plenty of smart, affordable talent to fill all those cubicles. However, two questions remain:

1. Can the next generation of students afford the same dream?
2. What will the masses of people without degrees do?

On the surface, the young look like incurable dependents. Later in the book, I'll talk about how they might end up fueling our next wave of innovation.

The Power of Intangibles

There's still some lubricant left in the U.S. innovation engine. As lopsided as things seem, the United States clings to a suite of intangibles that are as vital to American innovation as government support is to Europe or China.

Property Protection and Legal Structures

While imperfect, the U.S. legal system protects ideas, hard work, and investments better than most others. At its best, this system balances company profits with individual rights. Though it's been changing for the worse, U.S. law does typically, protects small business innovation from being crushed by the money and influence of powerful megacorporations.

Free Idea Exchange

Free speech and press are a counterbalance to the will of the powerful. Let's face it, there are things corrupt politicians or rich polluters would love for you not to know. Sometimes they succeed. But by allowing you to speak, write, and broadcast freely, the U.S. has a strong mechanism to drive change. That freedom combined with cheap, democratized communication tools can connect people and redirect capital in ways never before imaginable.

Companies like Kickstarter use those tools to help individuals raise awareness and investment for their projects. Others use them to bring competitive, open source ideas to life, like the Firefox browser, Wikipedia, and OpenOffice. Our advantage here won't last forever. The Internet is a great equalizer that will eventually free ideas even in the most repressed nations.

Immigration

The United States, more than most economies, has shown an ability to absorb and integrate immigrants. At the low end of the wage scale, there are laborers from poor Latin American countries. At the higher end, college students and industrious professionals come here from around the world to start businesses and employ people.

There is no better microcosm of this economic melting pot than the New York City taxi. The taxi became a gateway job for new immigrants coming to New York—Irish, Italian, Russian, Indian, African, and Middle Eastern. Whoever the new group was, it dominated the cab driver population for that period of time. As they learned the language and assimilated, they eventually moved on to higher paying jobs.

According to a study by the Manhattan Institute, some immigrants assimilate better than others. Table 2.1 shows the 2006

Table 2.1 Blending In

Country	Assimilation Index Score
Canada	53
Philippines	49
Cuba	43
Korea	41
Vietnam	41
All countries	28
China	21
El Salvador	18
India	16
Mexico	13

Source: www.mahattaninstitute.org/html/cr_53.htm.

assimilation index scores. (Higher numbers mean better economic, cultural, and civic assimilation.)

Our system obviously needs work, but it's superior to those of France and Germany, where vast populations of disenfranchised North Africans stand little chance of economic parity or an invitation to the Cannes Film Festival.

Open Trade

Despite our huge trade imbalances, it's good to know you can freely connect with suppliers around the world to make everything from smartphones to trade show tchotchkes come to life. At the very least, trade *into* the U.S. is relatively free. Outbound is a mixed bag. Large corporations, like GE and Boeing, make things other countries want, plus they command heaps of attention from government, which helps them export successfully. It's harder for smaller competitors to break into some protective Asian markets. South America is generally more receptive. All can require greasing the wheels to get things done. In the Capital Magnet chapter, I'll explore ways American innovators can thrive despite half-baked trade policies.

Intertwinement

Maybe the greatest luxury the United States has is its linkage to the rest of the world:

- We house some of the world's biggest companies and wealthiest people. Every global company drools at the site of an American consumer. They might mock our swagger or mismatched shorts-shirt combos, but they crave the luscious dollars bulging from our fanny packs.
- American culture still spreads like a fungus. We (the government?) threw babies, divorces, and weight problems at Britney Spears, but couldn't make a dent in her global success.
- Many countries rely on our aid or protection. Turkey, Israel, Central Europe, South Korea, Japan. They house our troops, take bundles of aid, and hide our dirty secrets. If times got really bad, we could at least count on a steady stream of affordable skewered meat and hummus.

Far too many entities have a stake in keeping the United States from falling too far too fast. The world demands its Britney Spears, but it won't wait forever to get something more valuable from the rest of us.

So What?

What is the value of an idea? If it produces a blog post, a song, or a movie, the answer might be zero. If that idea turns into something necessary, irresistible, and difficult to copy, the world will clamor for it. The United States is full of ideas and idea people. But the question remains: How many can thrive on services alone? As U.S. demographics show, the young are underutilized and the old are overextended. In between, those without a college education struggle to find employment—and purpose—in a digital world. The good news is that the situation is not going to stay that way. A deep financial hole is about to create conditions that are ripe with incentives and opportunity. Before diving deep into what innovators and entrepreneurs should do, Chapter 3 will explore what those economic conditions will be and how they'll transform U.S. business.

CHAPTER 3

The Next Decade

I read a blog post by Jeffrey Phillips referencing Martin Luther King and John F. Kennedy.* He wondered if Dr. King's "I Have a Dream" speech would have been as famous or effective if he used the word plan instead of dream. A plan seems like a bleak exercise done on spreadsheets while wearing charcoal gray slacks. But dreams can inspire. They set bold, impractical goals, like landing on the moon, ending Communism, or dating a supermodel. If the American Dream were a soufflé, its molten core would be filled with competitiveness, impracticality, charity, resilience, individuality, and idealism. Our cowboy spirit endures—long after the colonists, frontiersmen, gold rushers, John Wayne, and dot-com millionaires. That attitude might annoy Parisians as we rudely demand directions to the Louvre. But it's the same DNA that makes us see possibilities, start companies, and defy failure. It's an uncommon character that feels like it could singlehandedly end our economic problems.

I'd never underestimate the power of American ingenuity. After all, Americans have pioneered entire industries before—from Edison to the Wright brothers to Ford to Google to . . . okay, things slowed down about there. Still, the next boom could be right around the corner. It will create millions of jobs, revolutionize how we live, wipe out our debt and make Twix candy bars even more delicious. I want to believe that. Waiting for miracles is no way to run an economy. Businesses need both a dream *and* a plan. But a plan for what? This

---

*www.business-strategy-innovation.com/wordpress/2011/04/innovation-dreams-beat-innovation-plans.

chapter is all about what we can expect in the next 10 years and how it will impact innovation.

A Rebalancing: What's Likely, Possible, and Remote

My overall premise is simple: The next decade will be all about rebalancing. As we saw in the first couple of chapters, the United States had an incredibly long binge. The Great Recession was like *The Hangover*—we woke up in a place we didn't own, hadn't been to work for a while, and there was a raging tiger in the bathroom. The tiger, in this case, is Asia. That means U.S. innovators will face challenging conditions laden with opportunity. As in any battle with a feisty feline, there isn't much room for error.

Likely: Quasi-Invincible Sectors (a.k.a. "Necessities")

Let's start off with the good news. You are safe. That's right, I mean *you*. You're a power-suit-wearing professional with a haircut that obviously came from a salon, not a barbershop featuring an old, Italian immigrant with a shaky scissor hand. Or, you are a young tech dynamo, ready to accept your first million from a venture capitalist to build that killer start-up with a cute name, like krumb.el or kitch.in or krick.it. Though unemployment hovered around 9 percent in 2011, among your college-educated comrades it was only 5 percent. Even if that changed, you probably have enough LinkedIn connections to never have to eat sardines on toast. If you have kids, you'll insist they get a good education, or, at the very least, you'll come to terms with supporting their Hollywood dreams until Steven Spielberg calls and screams, "Enough!"

As in prior recessions, health, consumer staples (peanut butter, toilet paper), and utilities were unaffected. Manufacturing, which usually requires heavy commitments to land and equipment, lagged. Discretionary retail took a major hit. When the markets started to normalize, a purging took place. Weak competitors either right-sized or shut down. Companies like Best Buy got stronger as Circuit City and CompUSA disappeared. See Figure 3.1.

Telecom is an interesting beast. Because of how inseparable man and cell phone have become, telecom is now a consumer staple. I suspect most people would give up toilet paper or their children

	Entering recession	Exiting recession
1 — Health Care	Mixed	**Mostly led**
2 — Consumer Staples	Usually unaffected	**Usually unaffected**
2 — Utilities	Always unaffected	**Always unaffected**
3 — Materials	Either led or lagged	**Always lagged**
3 — Energy	Usually lagged	**Always lagged**
3 — Industrial	Mixed	**Mostly lagged**
4 — Consumer Discretionary	Always led	**Mixed**
4 — Telecom	Mostly led	**Mixed**
4 — Information Technology	Mostly led	**Mixed**
4 — Financials	Mixed	**Mixed**

Figure 3.1   Industry Decline and Recovery

Source: McKinsey.

before they part with their iPhone or high-speed Internet. For that same reason, technology, which is the pearl in America's oyster, also did well. Tech is also the main driver of automation, which explains its pervasiveness across every industry. It won't be long before your septic tank needs an IT department.

Even with an unimpressive recovery, energy will continue to bloom for three reasons: the search for renewable substitutes, government subsidies, and global demand. I know you've been worrying yourself sick about how Exxon Mobile and Shell will fare in the next decade. You can rest easy. Global demand for oil will keep prices high and black gold flowing—if not here, then in India and China. In the U.S., the push for energy independence will create lots of jobs searching for the holy grail of clean energy.

One sector that will not recover is real estate. The housing fiesta ended when the credit piñata burst. It took construction and home remodeling down with it. It will be a while before civil service workers can have columns in their atriums again. Finance, too, will be smaller, but no less profitable as it's all hands on deck to look for the next bubble.

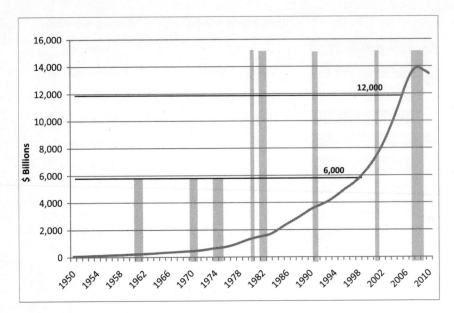

Figure 3.2   U.S. Household Debt 1950–2010

Note: Shaded areas represent U.S. recessions.

Source: U.S. Federal Reserve.

Likely: Financial Shrinkage and the End of Easy Credit

Most of the financial services industry grew because of debt, complexity, and bad governmental parenting. If you look at Figure 3.2, you can see how for 35 years household debt spread like gossip at an Oscars party. It became normal to buy a home that took 30 years to pay off, and then take a second mortgage on it. Government incentives helped. Many of these financial distortions will soon go away.

Fewer, Shorter Loans   People will still want big houses, but borrowed money will be harder to get. New laws have been introduced to reduce lending predators, the ones in gray vans with tinted windows and "Wachovia Rules!" bumper stickers. Fannie and Freddie were weakened by the mortgage crisis and might wither away. If they do, home ownership will again be limited to those who can afford it. We'll start seeing banks actually bearing the risk for the mortgages they issue, instead of packaging and reselling them. These loans will have shorter durations (15 or 20 years not 30) and require a 20 to 30 percent down payment. This will drive down the cost of housing, since fewer can afford these terms. About 67 percent of Americans own homes, compared with 46 percent in Germany and 37 percent in Switzerland. In other words, our number will drop, but we'll live.

Surplus Real Estate   Home prices will eventually stabilize, but the United States will be sitting on piles of surplus properties in places no one wants to live. Parts of Florida and Detroit have no people but lots of homes that could be repurposed in creative ways. New York City started converting unused land into enterprise zones where the city provides start-ups with discounted office space and even administrative support in exchange for potential commerce. New York City also took huge swaths of unused waterfront property—old warehouses, train yards—and opened them up to commercial and housing development.

Protected by Complexity   Finally, complexity is not going away. New laws and regulations will be introduced, as will new agencies to manage and botch future crises. What I don't see happening is the government fanning the flames of competition. More regulation only ensures megacorporations will be the only ones that can afford the cost of compliance. It's happening already. In 2007, financial services employed only 8 million out of a national workforce of 114 million, but made 27 percent of all corporate profits. By 2010, the industry shed about one million jobs, but its share of profits went up to 31 percent.

Shifting Focus of Innovation   There is too much money at stake for the financial industry to sit still. Since financial data is infinitely digital and all data eventually becomes financial, there will be countless ways to turn information gathered from mobile phones, shoppers, and social networks into profits. As new regulations focus on borrowing, innovation will shift from borrowers to savers, investors, and businesses. Small business financing is especially ripe with opportunity . . . and the makings of another bubble. Unless the United States finds its rhythm, most financing will flow into fast growing emerging markets. Domestic production might offer enough domestic returns to keep some of that capital here.

If growth in financial services remains modest, there is a good chance we'll see some of the top minds formerly drawn to alchemy go into productive fields that generate tangible benefits to society. Famed investor Jim Rogers, who moved to Singapore and taught his kids Chinese, tends to eat his own cooking as an investor and a citizen. He thinks the next superstars will be farmers, not financial wizards. We'll see. Personally, I hope it'll be business book authors.

Possible: Crisis Part II—Shaky Demand for U.S. Debt, Inflation, and Possible Default

"It's our currency, but it's your problem."
—*John Connally, treasury secretary under Richard M. Nixon*

Super-Fed   Many of the United States' risks become a bit less scary when you consider our money situation. Sure, we owe more than all other troubled economies combined. But we have one talent Greece, Ireland, and Spain don't—alchemy. I'm talking about the Federal Reserve. The Fed, as its friends call it, is an incredibly complicated and powerful beast. It's a public-private hybrid that controls our monetary system, and according to conspiracy buffs, space and time. It's true that the Fed has many mysterious powers. That's why people like Congressman Ron Paul want to dismantle it, or, at the very least, peek under its skirt. For now, the most important thing to know is the Fed sets interest rates and controls money supply. That's the fancy way of saying "poof" and making money appear. It can do this because:

1. By lending cheaply to banks, the Fed can make private lending profitable even at low rates. That injects money into the economy like a baster injects gravy into a turkey. That can help businesses grow. When too much is injected, it can also create stock or housing bubbles. An overcooked turkey, if you will.
2. Since 2008, The Fed can simply make money and credit it to banks. They're just numbers, not massive shipments of paper.
3. It can buy U.S. debt, which it has done a lot of lately. The United States needs money. It could pay private investors or China 5 percent on a 10-year bond or it could sell it "at auction" to the Fed for 3.5 percent. This is a great way to pay your bills, until it isn't. History is littered with failed paper currencies and we're treading a fine line.

4. The Fed can lower bank reserve requirements so banks can keep less money in the vault, lending more of it out. (Though there is nothing forcing them to do that.)
5. The Fed can buy toxic assets directly from banks through open market operations. This was how TARP worked. The government replaced bad mortgage loans with nice, friendly treasury notes.

You can see in Figure 3.3, the Fed has been hyperactive in recent years, infusing reserve funds into the economy. That kind of intervention is a sign of how dire the situation became and how badly banks needed capital. Even as cash flowed in, large, safe companies got loans they didn't need. Eventually, all that printed cash should find its way to small business. The question the coming chapters will answer is: Where should that next wave of entrepreneurs place their bets?

Under-Fed   The Fed will have less creative license than in the two years since the recession. As our credit ratings drop, it will cost the United States more to borrow than Germany, Australia, or Canada. The

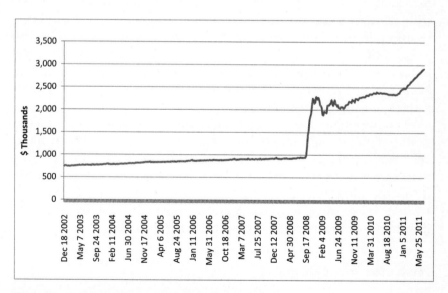

Figure 3.3   Increasing Supply of Reserve Funds by the Fed
Source: U.S. Federal Reserve.

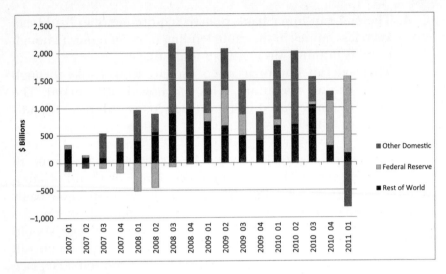

Figure 3.4   Who's Funding the U.S. Budget Deficit?
Source: U.S. Federal Reserve.

good news is, we're still beating the pants off Sudan and North Korea. With almost $10 trillion owed to private lenders and $4.6 trillion owed to government agencies for Medicare and the Fed's swanky new swimming pool, there are reasons to worry. If rates were to go up by 2 percent, in less than five years we'd add over $200 billion in annual interest payments. That's plenty of incentive to keep printing dollars at the expense of savers hungry for higher interest on their retirement money.

Fed impotence could turn our creditors into comic book villains as they demand high rates to buy our debt and dates with our finest celebrities. Already, demand for U.S. debt is teetering. In 2009, the Fed bought 80 percent of U.S. bonds. In the fourth quarter of 2010, it did the same. Unless growth picks up, in the next 10 years the United States will pay much higher rates to borrow from private investors—or risk rampant inflation. See Figure 3.4.

Possible: New Reserve Currency

Good Dollar   The dollar is the Scotch Tape keeping our complicated financial scheme from imploding, here's how:

- U.S. treasuries are the most widely held financial instrument in the world, so few have an interest in watching its value crumble or dumping their holdings. China, which holds almost $2 trillion, has the most to lose. Of course, if enough money is made from thin air, we can eventually let China print its own U.S. bonds from the comfort of its living room.
- Most commodities like oil and crops are priced in dollars. So are futures contracts. That creates demand for dollars.
- Many world currencies are tied to ours, including the Chinese yuan. When the dollar was linked to gold and the United States was growing, this made sense. Now that we have an incentive to inflate our debt away, it would be complicated, but not impossible for countries to unpeg from the dollar.
- The struggling euro, which has taken share from the dollar in global transactions, is in limbo. Germany and to some extent, France, are bailing out Greece, Ireland, Spain, and other troubled European Union members. Without another abundant, independent, third currency, the dollar remains a player, if only by attrition.

It's hard to say how long this can hold up. As long as it does, the U.S. has time to right its finances. Still, the seams are starting to show. China has practically stopped buying new U.S. debt in favor of gold, raw materials, and several Greek islands and souvlaki stands.

Bad Dollar   Our frenzy to get out of debt is not going unnoticed. Like a bumbling movie killer digging a ditch in broad daylight, we're having a hard time keeping the bodies buried. By 2010, it became clear the United States was printing money. Leaders from Brazil and other countries criticized us for an irresponsible flood of cash that caused global food, stock, and real estate prices to skyrocket. That's why the dollar's decline as reserve currency has gotten lots of momentum. Consider the following:

- From 2000 to 2008, the dollar already dropped from 71 percent to 64 percent of world reserves. Most of that was from the popularity of the euro.
- Bill Gross, manager of the world's biggest bond fund, pointed out that when chaos exploded in the Middle East in 2011,

money poured into precious metals, not treasuries, which used to be safe havens for frightened investors.

- In 2011, China, Brazil, Russia, India, and oil-producing countries decided to trade with each other in their own currencies, not U.S. dollars.
- The Organization of Arab Petroleum Exporting Countries (OAPEC) agreed on a five-year plan to create its own currency.

While I don't think the dollar will disappear that quickly, demand for it will take a big hit. After all, even Sophia Loren didn't have as many suitors in 2010 as she did in 1967. I'd imagine her numbers would be worse if she also had a raging cupcake addiction. Some are already starting to innovate away from dollars into new and uncharted currency alternatives.

Borderless Bitcoins: Bitcoin attracted a lot of attention. It's the world's first decentralized, open source, anonymous digital currency. I know that's a mouthful. Basically, Bitcoin is a "mined" digital currency that promises to limit inflation by carefully controlling the growth in supply at a reasonable rate. Like any digital currency, it's easy for online stores to accept. It also attracted some passionate early adopters like computer geeks, armchair revolutionaries, and conspiracy theorists.

Unlike anything else before it, it also attracted the ire of government leaders like Senator Charles Schumer, who claimed it could be used nefariously (like dollars?). While it might not endure, Bitcoin points the way to a global currency that cannot be manipulated by individuals or governments. Something that powerful will either be crushed by powerful interests or become unstoppable, like a supermodel on a good hair day.

Hard Alternative Currency: Stan Stalnaker of Hub Culture has created a global digital currency called the Ven. The Ven is backed by a basket of currencies, commodities, and precious metals. Stan's ambitious vision is to create the first independent global currency that can be traded digitally or in the real world. In June 2011, banks began purchasing Ven. Stan expects this alternate economy to pass 1 billion Ven by 2012.

Panda Bonds: McDonald's is also hedging its bets against the dollar. In Hong Kong, the company started issuing bonds in Chinese yuan, not dollars. As China opens its financial markets more, this will become more common. After all, Sophia Loren just had another cupcake.

Productive Dollar   Not only will a cheap dollar help U.S. exports and reduce debt, it will change the rules of innovation. An economy built for consumption suddenly finds itself with the will, if not the skill, to produce. Even if we do begin to produce, currency shifts will demand changes in pricing strategies, long-term contracts, where companies locate their operations, and how they invest.

Likely: Surpluses and Scarcities—China Wants Porterhouses, Too

Global competition is about to go through a major shift. The stage is set for a showdown between consumers in the West and emerging ones in the Far East. China has been patiently biding its time, keeping wages low and its currency depressed for a good reason: Nobody likes an overly cheerful currency. Actually, the Chinese have been building their savings and increasing productive capacity on the back of our consumption and borrowing. Money they previously held in treasuries is now buying natural resources in Africa and elsewhere. See Figure 3.5.

As demand in the West slows down, Chinese consumers (and to some extent, Brazilian and Indian ones) are ready to roar . . . into shopping malls. To keep factories humming, the Chinese will replace foreign customers with domestic ones (decoupling from Western economies). They'll do that by letting their currency float higher against the dollar. Suddenly, those long hours at the factory will all seem worth it. Chinese will wear their finest Calvin Kleins as they drag Ikea furniture into their newly remodeled apartments. Their bellies will be full of delicious Kobe beef, sea urchins, and dried fish candy (yes, it's true).

There are 1.4 billion Chinese, thousands of whom enter the middle class daily. This will create competition for every type of natural resource. Steaks, gadgets, and cars are made from finite resources, not Angry Birds. China's new wealth will raise prices or create scarcity across the spectrum of materials—from oil to

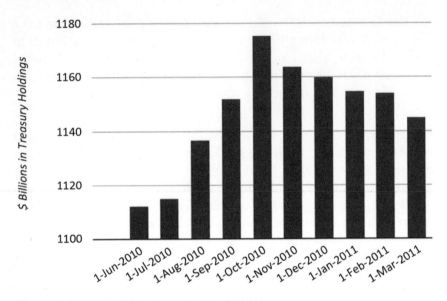

Figure 3.5   Chinese Find Other Places for Their Money

Source: Treasury International Capital Monthly Reports.

metals to grains. On the plus side, scarcity will drive global innovation opportunities in recycling, efficiency, substitution, and
conservation.

On this side of the world, consumer demand in Asia and Latin
America will mean using a weaker dollar to pay for pricier phones
and lawn gnomes. In 2010, fuel, food, and materials prices rose over
20 percent in the U.S. and more around the world. As it gets more
expensive to ship things here, it's easy to imagine Chinese consumers being first to get the newest iPads. Higher shipping costs and
rising wages might also help make new forms of domestic production viable. More on that later.

Not everything will get more expensive. Housing, which is the
biggest expense for most, should stay flat or get cheaper—especially
if you don't mind living in Detroit or Florida swampland.
Overdevelopment and slow population growth will keep prices in
check. Places like New York, San Francisco, Austin, and Salt Lake
City that have lots of culture, jobs, and flamboyant decorators will
maintain their caché. As baby boomers age, they will enter their
spend-down years. That means more demand for in-home entertainment but less for home furnishings, minivans, and surfboards.

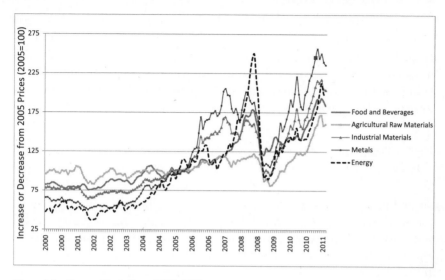

Figure 3.6   Commodity Indices, 2000–2011

Source: International Monetary Fund, World Economic Outlook, April 2011.

Likely: Big Cuts, Taxes, and Reallocation of Resources

Fears of higher borrowing costs and a damaged dollar finally are pressuring politicians to act like adults. The next decade will feature a leaner, possibly meaner, government. When President Obama's bipartisan commission came back with sensible cuts and tax increases, their ideas were immediately ignored. As evidenced by the debt ceiling spat in the summer of 2011, deep down everyone knows we'll eventually have to swallow the medicine. Hopefully, it will be us holding the spoon, not our creditors. Below are just a few of the big changes to expect.

Changes to Entitlements   Changes to entitlements mean restructuring Social Security, Medicare, and Medicaid. First, the wealthy will have to pay for themselves and likely subsidize low-wage earners. It remains to be seen what the government considers wealthy. My guess would be $250,000—just enough for a small apartment in Manhattan or a castle in Afghanistan. Since people practically live forever now, a higher retirement age is inevitable. To make a difference, it will need to move from 67 to at least 70 in the next 15 years.

As people become entitled to fewer, um, entitlements, fear and uncertainly will wash over the masses as never before. For innovation, fear means an opportunity to offer security. For others, the absence of a safety net can be a liberation of sorts. It will force a small, but productive segment of the population to start businesses and try to outpace the crushing health and education costs.

Big Tax Hikes   The Bush tax cuts on dividends, capital gains, and estates will likely be eliminated. Beyond that, how high can (or should) taxes go? To illustrate the magnitude of our problem, consider Figure 3.7. Just to pay off the $8.7 trillion of budget deficits (not debt!) projected from 2008 to 2013, the United States would need to raise the average tax rate for all citizens to 66 percent over the next 10 years. To pay it off over 20 years, that rate would have to be 53 percent. That doesn't even touch the existing national debt.

Cuts in Education   As Federal tuition loans and public school budgets shrink, there will be pressure to privatize. This will open countless

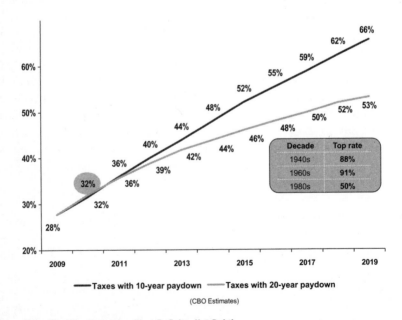

Figure 3.7   Tax Hike Scenarios (New Deficits, Not Debt)

Source: Congressional Budget Office, Bureau of Labor Statistics, Bureau of Economic Analysis.

opportunities for private companies to offer entirely new kinds of education—at a profit. I'll get to the specifics later in the book.

Likely: Battle of the States

When it comes to financial mismanagement, the states could teach the federal government a trick or two. At least the Fed can create money. States have mastered finance in ways that only a Latin American dictator could appreciate. For years, many resorted to accounting tricks to calculate pensions, selling roads to close budget gaps, or issuing bonds to pay salaries. Most already sold the naming rights to every public facility. It was just a matter of time before "I live in Pepsi" or "Just moved here from Cisco" would seem like perfectly normal sentences.

The recession left many states with high unemployment payouts, but huge drops in property and income tax revenues. In 2010, Illinois—one of the most corrupt and poorly run states—practically shut down before politicians finally agreed to raise taxes by as much as 75 percent. Across all states, shortfalls totaled $130 billion in 2011, but are projected to drop to $75 billion in 2013. States like New York, New Jersey, California, and Texas will each have over $10 billion in shortfalls going into 2013. See Figure 3.8.

The recession exposed another goiter that was about to get bigger than the patient. As private sector salaries and benefits shrank,

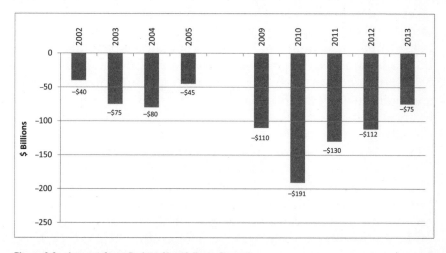

Figure 3.8   Largest State Budget Shortfalls on Record

Source: Center on Budget and Policy Priorities (CBPP).

state and local governments blissfully ignored the trend. Government employees could work for 25 years, retire at 50, and keep getting health care and most of their final year's salary (juiced up by overtime) forever! Good thing all the immortals work for Marvel Comics, not New Jersey. For the foreseeable future, most states sit on services they can't afford and union salaries that are 60 percent higher than in the private sector. New Jersey, for example, could be in a $150 billion hole, if it calculated pensions the way private businesses do. I can't say I'm thrilled that government gets to have an entirely separate branch of mathematics to calculate pensions.

No matter how you look at it, bus fares will go up, public schools will do without fresh broccoli or books, and you'll wait a lot longer for your glamorous driver's license photo. Budget gaps will breed opportunities for business:

- Cost savings and efficiency solutions for government
- Private sector alternatives for missing government services—they helped will be the biggest
- Tax, toll, enforcement, and fee collection technologies
- Pension alternatives
- Incentives for private sector jobs to replace public sector ones

Many states are getting desperate and aggressive. Some have been underestimating declines in home values to keep property taxes as high as possible. They've always fought tooth and nail for tourist dollars, shoppers, and sports franchises. In some cases, they helped finance stadiums or malls to generate tax revenues. When Illinois announced 75 percent tax increases, Governor Christie of New Jersey did not waste any time offering companies tax breaks and unlimited access to Jon Bon Jovi. Businesses will have lots of leverage in the next 10 years. I wouldn't be surprised if some states subsidized worker salaries or even changed the lyrics to "Livin' on a Prayer" in honor of your company. "Livin' on a Prius"??

Think I'm exaggerating? Kansas offered AMC Theaters a 10-year tax abatement to relocate from neighboring Missouri. This is a zero-sum game for the United States and ultimately, a race to the bottom. A better use of resources (and the only good use of stimulus dollars) would be to offer foreign manufacturers deals to produce here. Ideal targets would be companies with sales growth, high complexity products, a supplier ecosystem, and high global demand potential.

We could offer them land, tax abatements, and Barbara Streisand. I kid. She's a treasure.

Possible: Revenues from the Fringe

Have you rummaged through the wallet of a California resident lately? If you have, one thing you're likely to find is a medical marijuana card. Yes, the same person you've known for years who's never stubbed a toe or popped a zit suddenly has glaucoma and chronic back spasms. California is running an experiment that's likely to spread across the entire country. It's called taxation. They've decriminalized and taxed a substance that is statistically safer than booze but has the stigma of hard drugs. Governor Cuomo of New York is already studying the issue, presumably under the strict supervision of Dr. Snoop Dog.

There's big money in decriminalization. In 2008, Harvard economist Jeffrey Miron estimated that drug legalization would bring in almost $77 billion a year. That includes $44 billion from law enforcement savings and the rest from tax revenues. Of course, Mr. Miron included hard drugs. It remains to be seen which states are willing to get that experimental. At the federal level, decriminalization would free up resources that enrich the least productive segments of society: terrorists, private prison companies, lawyers, and Mexican drug dealers who've made police beheadings that country's top sport.

Drug legalization won't be the first place governments look for new taxes, but they will look. Somewhere deep in the bowels of a cash-strapped Texas town there's at least one politician considering gay marriage—as a revenue stream. As always, cigarettes and alcohol will see higher taxes. Online gambling, casinos, even prostitution might get a second look. Who knows, Arizona might decide to give Nevada a run for its money in the sin department. Of course, these are all easy fixes. Our future lies in creating businesses that grow and employ lots of people productively, not seductively.

Possible: Capital and Talent Flight

A Duke University study showed that immigrants are responsible for 25 percent of start-ups in the U.S. With tighter visa restrictions and a struggling economy, many budding entrepreneurs might never make it here. Similarly, the ones already here can leave. I don't think this will happen in big batches, but I do think a sour economy creates a flight risk.

At some companies in Hong Kong, the number of resumes coming from the United States has gone up by 20 to 30 percent. This is just anecdotal, but the implication is real. We have a service workforce that isn't tied down to factories and infrastructure. People with money, education, or connections can leave. And they will, if taxes get too high or opportunities get too sparse. (If they try, I wouldn't be surprised to see the federal government impose punitive taxes on those departing.)

There's also involuntary job flight. That's where the jobs leave but the people stay. Economist Alan Blinder, who wrote one of my pricey economics textbooks at New York University, estimated that another 22 percent of U.S. jobs are vulnerable to off-shoring. Many of these are high-paying professions ranging from finance to science to *American Idol* judge. Presumably, some are also economists.

The bright side is that other countries are far worse off. Their failures might prove to be our opportunity. Consider Bain & Company's survey of 2,500 wealthy Chinese, 57 percent of whom have contemplated emigration. Of those who thought about leaving, 10 percent filed papers. Another 33 percent were sick of fish-flavored snacks and craved an occasional crusty baguette. (Okay, I made up that last part.) Wealthy Indians are notorious for stashing money overseas. What if we offered them tax-free, confidential returns in every investment in a U.S.-based small business? Shhh . . . you didn't hear me say that.

Probable: Innovation Stimulation

Originally, I was against the government's rescue of Ford. With hindsight as my guide, rolling the dice to restructure a big domestic manufacturer was a smart move. Even the chance of saving a self-sustaining enterprise beats knowing thousands might be unemployed indefinitely.

If you have a company that can be considered of strategic importance nationally or locally, you're in luck—the government is looking for investments. We are witnessing the start of a more proactive, even desperate government. I expect huge amounts of borrowed dollars to pour into innovation incentives. Some of it will come from cuts in existing subsidies for agriculture and oil. That's exactly what the EU is doing. Europe is unwinding a long history of agricultural subsidies to plow that money into scientific research, hopefully to engineer even better Croissants. Below are some likely recipients of U.S. government cash.

The Military   This is one of the country's big-ticket expenses. We'll shift from jets, tanks, and lots of soldiers to a tech-intensive video game model where doughy kids control expensive drones as military moms stock up on Skittles to sustain them. Ironically, it's the same strategy Donald Rumsfeld got criticized for. Military suppliers aren't going to let their good relationships go to waste. Instead of cuts, government dollars will shift toward DARPA, the Defense Department's successful, independent R&D unit. It will fund technologies like cybercrime, encryption, robotics, spy equipment, impervious wireless networks, and remote-controlled automation. We will not see as many giant plane, tank, and submarine budgets, unless Al Qaeda starts a navy.

Green Energy, Health, and Technology   With legislation like the $8.6 billion America COMPETES Act, the government will likely spend lots more money on scientific research in green energy, health, and technology. It's unclear how well these investments will do as they're poured through thick bureaucracies with competing agendas. Plus, the money that comes out often has strings attached.

Start-up or Corporate Tax Incentives   Other incentives might come in the form of start-up funds or corporate tax breaks. While these can be effective for small companies, many of the largest corporations already pay virtually no taxes due to loopholes or Bermuda holding companies. Corporate taxes are less than 9 percent of overall U.S. tax revenue, so this "lever" is more of a nub.

Direct Subsidies   As the tax lever disappears, tax breaks turn into tax subsidies. I expect significant investment in fostering domestic manufacturing. Although the government isn't always the best investor, this is a far better use of tax money than missiles or retail stimulus. This trend has already begun. Dow Kokam received over $340 million in both federal and Michigan tax dollars to open its Detroit battery plant.

Definite: Distortions

As economic policies and innovation dance awkwardly in the pale moonlight, there are quite a few ghosts in our machine that will influence this relationship. A 2010 study by Corruption Perceptions Index (no, I did not make that up) ranks Singapore, Denmark, and New Zealand as the least corrupt countries. All three scored over 9 on a 10-point scale.*

The U.S. had a respectable 7.1. By comparison, the average survey participant in Brazil (3.7), Russia (2.1), India (2.1), and China (3.5) missed out on $45 in bribes while filling out the form. Sadly, low corruption does not automatically equal competence. For a variety of reasons, listed in the next section, the United States still ends up with more than its share of policies that distort behaviors, create odd incentives, and create boom and bust cycles.

Influence for Sale   In the Third World, we seem to think there's something crude and unseemly about passing an envelope filled with $5,000 under a table to a government official. Sure, your construction contract gets approved, but you might want to take a hot shower afterward. Yet in the U.S., we think nothing of hundred-thousand-dollar corporate donations to candidates or political action committees. Somehow, it seems cleaner, more dignified. It even has a prettier name: lobbying. Say that 10 times in a row. It sounds like a soothing lullaby. Try that with "bribery." It's like an alarm blaring heavy metal at 5:00 A.M.

I wouldn't call it bribery, but influence is all about perception. It's hard to be perceived as independent when the only way to get into office is to raise massive amounts of cash. The motivations of donors vary, but I'd imagine few believe big money has no strings. Ever get a $100,000 gift from a total stranger whom you never saw again? Table 3.1 shows the staggering expense of getting elected to a public office in the United States.

Despite talk of campaign finance reform, few incumbents have an incentive to change the system that gave them subservient interns, free health care, and a regular spot on *Meet the Press*. So, the arms race continues. By 2012, it will cost $1 billion to become president. No matter how noble the candidate, it's hard to imagine raising that

---

*www.transparency.org/policy_research/surveys_indices/cpi/2010.

Table 3.1   The Costs of Getting Elected

Year	Candidate	Amount Spent	Items Purchased
2010	All Candidates	$4B	Primaries, conventions, spending by the parties and outsiders
2008		$2.8B	
2004		$1.9B	
2012	Barack Obama	$1B (projected)	Presidency
2012	Republican Presidential Candidate	$700M (projected)	
2008	Barack Obama	$750M	
2008	John McCain	$333M	Earlier retirement
2004	George W. Bush	$367M	Presidency
2004	John Kerry	$310M	Media and PR
2010	Meg Whitman	$179M	
2010	Michael Bloomberg	$108M	New York mayor and term limits suspension

kind of dough without owing a few favors. On the flip side, there are independently wealthy candidates like Michael Bloomberg and Meg Whitman who spend their own millions to get elected . . . or at least, try. It's a strange and tainted system that can produce anything from an incompetent patsy to a benevolent dictator. Dependence on money with strings is not a recipe for representative government or sound economic decisions; it's a puppet show.

In 2010, influence got supersized as the Supreme Court gave corporations the same rights as actual humans to contribute to candidates and political groups. Shortly after the decision, companies showered $300 million on candidates. Corporations dwarf all others in spending power, but unions and other special interests are no strangers to the influence game. The only outcasts are the moderate majority, who tend not to organize. If you don't pick a team, you're not dining with the Senator.

The Spawn of Influence, Revisited   Buckets of cash have a way of creating distortions that lumber through our economy with all the grace of the Stay Puft Marshmallow Man from *Ghostbusters*. As a result, some industries get special perks and privileges. Here are just a few examples:

Industry Subsidies: Created in 1921, when 25 percent of the United States was agrarian, farm subsidies might have made sense. Today, sophisticated corporate farms receive $20 billion a year from the U.S. government for corn, wheat, and other staple crops. The oversupply explains why almost everything, possibly even this book, is made of high fructose corn syrup. Oil companies also get a helping hand—about $4 billion a year. Some do have green logos . . .

Big Contracts: The wars in Iraq and Afghanistan generated some big, no-bid contracts for several companies. One of the most successful, Halliburton, had previously been managed by Vice President Dick Cheney. On the state level, New York spawned a cottage industry of former politicians lobbying for investment firms to get a piece of the state's pension fund.

High-Fee Financial Accounts: As funded pensions disappeared, employers and the financial industry successfully lobbied for a heap of self-funded alternatives: IRA, 401(k), 529 Plans, health savings accounts, and flexible spending accounts. These can be valuable savings instruments, but too many have huge fees. Basically, they transfer wealth from consumers to financial companies. In 2010, President Obama promoted the benefits of high fee annuities. Ten years earlier, George W. Bush proposed allowing people to invest their Social Security dollars in stocks. That would have been interesting . . .

Distortions Mentioned Earlier: Bush tax cuts for the wealthy, financial deregulation, creation of Fannie and Freddie to guarantee home loans, the North American Free Trade Agreement (NAFTA), credits for exporting jobs, and free passes for architects of the Great Recession all qualify as distortions.

It's amusing when I hear someone wax poetic about preserving "capitalism" or our "market economy." As companies scratch and crawl over each other for tax breaks, bailouts, and favoritism, I wonder are we really *that* different from China, Russia, or other distorted economies? Favoritism and distortions aren't going anywhere. A few egregious ones, like farm subsidies, will likely go away. Others will linger in the shadows, unless economic turmoil casts a bright light their way. I think we'll land somewhere short of turmoil. Even in malaise, small businesses can start to get the kind of attention from government typically reserved for megacorporations. What's already starting to happen is that entrepreneurs are forming informal support networks. Some of these networks could evolve to wield influence the way unions once did for employees. Why is that valuable? Historically, it's small business that grows an economy, not megacorps. Their influence is already felt far, wide, and deep in America's pockets.

Remote: Collapse and the Revenge of Mystery Meat?

Remember going to your school cafeteria as a kid and wondering what that brown meat-like loaf was? I don't know if eating it made me brave or stupid. Either way, I lived to write about it. Strangely, I get the same feeling when I invest in stocks or put money in a bank account. The *Guardian* published a breakdown of the global asset bubble created leading up to the recession. It's staggering to think that the value of all things that existed on the planet in 2007 was only $55 trillion, but the value of financial assets (many on the books of global banks) was $290 trillion. See Figure 3.9.

With bailouts, money printing, and romantic interludes between banks and government, it's hard to say what's changed. Doom and

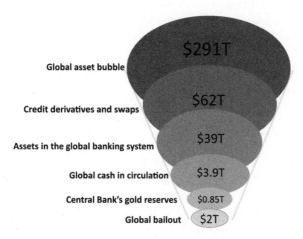

Figure 3.9   Global Asset Bubble
Source: The Guardian.

gloomers would say "not much" and expect another, bigger collapse. Even sensible investors, like Mark Mobius, executive chairman of Templeton Asset Management, believe that another crisis is inevitable. He has a point. Little was resolved last time. In the long term, there are still too many kids at school eating this mystery meat. It may not be delicious—or even food—but it's not in anyone's interest to poison the students. If you do believe a collapse of that magnitude is coming, please put down this book. Stock your farm with guns, booze, smokes, and gold. Add a few cans of mystery meat and wait. You'll emerge from the apocalypse equal parts *Road Warrior* and Warren Buffett.

A Shift in Power, Capital, and Priorities

All this belt tightening is making it hard to enjoy my second helping of KFC. The next decade will have plenty of delicious fried chicken and jobs frying it. Those jobs probably won't put a child through college or buy health insurance for the inevitable angioplasty. At the same time, the college kids using that KFC for a little midnight fuel will have a world of opportunity at their fingertips. As they leave grease marks all over their new Android phones, they'll plot the next digital revolution—likely something that will make it even more difficult to care about their boring, analog families.

The next decade will start with a gimpy U.S. consumer (see Figure 3.10). With the credit binge gone, higher taxes, health costs, and flat wages will keep Mr. Jones from buying a third flat screen for the bathroom. Similarly, government is running low on options to keep us competitive. What remains is an empowered, wealthy, private sector that can chase profits to the farthest, dustiest corners of New Delhi.

Wheelchairs or Roller Coasters?

Imagine a huge country with abundant resources that in the last decade could only muster new jobs in one industry: health care. As baby boomers come to terms with smaller pensions and early-bird specials, masses of uninsured will soon get health coverage. Our fixation on health costs the U.S. almost $8,000 per person a year but buys a lower life expectancy than countries spending less than half that. The numbers will get even higher as baby boomers retire.

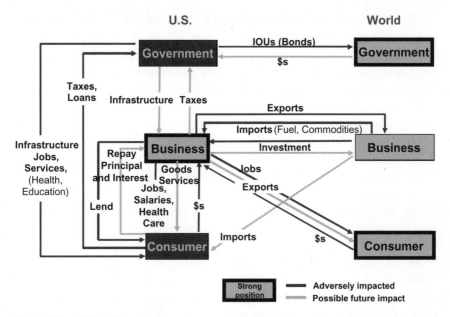

Figure 3.10   Shifting Balance of Power

What's important to remember is health care is a consumptive industry. The health industry is built on preservation and defense, not
risk-taking and offense. Yes, some medical innovations can be
exported, but the vast majority of the work is maintenance. To thrive
again, the United States needs more than mechanics, it needs people
who build the machines. And over the next few years, economic
conditions will finally make that possible.

What exactly are these possibilities? The rest of *Econovation*
explores the five opportunity themes for the next decade. Some are
directly driven by the trends discussed earlier. Others will merely
succeed because of them. Each is loaded with actionable ideas,
unexpected examples, and one too many anecdotes. The five
themes are:

1. **Chapter 4: Sell Actualization.** Things changed after the recession. Consumers took on weary, post-recession psychology
   that many companies have yet to fully understand or profit
   from. Aging, economic uncertainty, and career concerns will
   force companies to sell and operate differently to tap into that
   new psychology. The weary American consumer still hungers
   for possessions, but fewer and with meaning this time.

2. **Chapter 5: Build a Capital Magnet.** Macro forces will ultimately force the reigning champions of consumption to attract customers and cash from abroad. Building a capital magnet is no easy task, but the conditions are ripe for U.S. companies to produce things they can export and capitalize on emerging market growth in ways they never thought possible.

3. **Chapter 6: Make Makers.** A nation of producers, or "makers," needs a smarter, slimmer, and more productive generation of doers, not diners. I'll talk about how businesses and individuals can make it so.

4. **Chapter 7: Micropreneurship.** A breed walks among us that is slightly different, more adventurous, more willing to take risks to start businesses that change the world. There are countless opportunities to help makers unlock their potential. Once its unlocked, only they can create the jobs, customers, and tax revenues to save an atrophied economy.

5. **Chapter 8: Incentive Nation.** Finally, businesses will need to know how to wield micro incentives, to motivate domestic consumers and employees in a stagnant, saturated economy.

So What?

Table 3.2 sums up all the likely possible and remote events discussed in this chapter. I realize the danger of providing such a handy

Table 3.2   Rebalancing for the Future

Likely	• Quasi-invincible sectors
	• Innovation stimulation
	• Financial shrinkage
	• Higher commodity prices/decoupling
	• Big cuts, taxes, and reallocation of resources
	• Battle of the states
	• Distortions
	• A shift in power, capital, and priorities
Possible	• New reserve currency
	• Crisis II
	• Revenues from the fringe
	• Capital and talent flight
Remote	• Collapse and the Revenge of Mystery Meat?

summary. A decade from now, you'll only need this one page for us to have a lively debate about the clarity or disrepair of my crystal ball. Of course, that's not the point of all this. My goal is to prepare innovators for the conditions that lie ahead and help them decide which ideas will prosper and which will fail.

As we'll see in the next chapter, the American consumer will not be the centerpiece of most successful ideas. The American producer will. To appreciate what I mean by that, let's jump into "Sell Actualization."

4

Sell Actualization

Y ou're probably familiar with Maslow's hierarchy of needs (Figure 4.1). At the bottom, the pyramid starts with the basics—food, clothing, shelter, sex. Then you move on to safety, love and belonging, esteem, and finally self-actualization. In Maslow's view, people realize their full potential through invention, self-expression, and creativity.

Toward the end of the twentieth century, it seemed like Americans finally earned the leisure time, money, and tools to self-actualize. Many did. They raised smart kids, built companies, or found ways to let their true talents flourish. But the majority borrowed, shopped, and actualized their way right into recession. Maslow didn't spend years rejecting other, inferior polygons so we could screw up his perfect pyramid. Could the pyramid be wrong? Or, did the spoils of leisure make us lose sight of what really drives actualization and fulfillment—work itself. And I don't mean *all* work. Ever meet someone who makes a piece of jewelry or furniture? They'll spend hours showing it off, explaining the contours, and sharing their techniques. They produced something. Many lawyers, financiers, and PowerPoint jockeys rarely feel the same way. In the downturn, people who lost their jobs realized how much of their identity was based on those jobs. Even the ones who remained employed began to reevaluate the meaning, or lack of it, in their professional lives.

The Seven Economic Identities

Selling actualization is about people, not consumers. Our economic identity is rooted in what we do, not what we purchase. A company that helps you save $100 on a laptop will not be as valuable as one

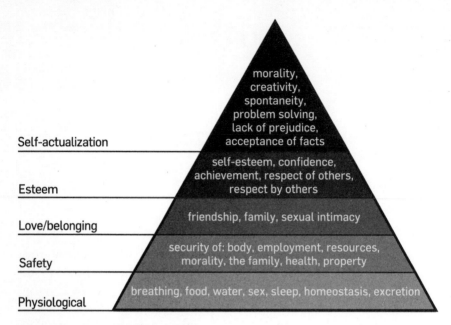

Figure 4.1   Maslow's Hierarchy of Needs

that helps you become more marketable. If that same investment of time can earn you an extra $5,000 a year, you'll never have to worry about the $100. The emerging opportunity for business is to help people become better, not save $100. There are lots of ways to tap into this emerging desire for purpose. Much of it has to do with how employers redefine work for a fulfillment-starved labor pool. Selling actualization and evoking a sense of productive purpose will be at the heart of every business opportunity I explore in *Econovation*.

Whether viewed as employees or domestic consumers, my research shows seven economic identities starting to emerge. People's identity is strongly tied to their financial condition, earning potential, and aspirations. See Table 4.1.

Get Your Free Labor Here!

The single biggest part of actualization is *where it happens*. Climbers, Libertines, and Tech Turks often derive a greater sense of meaning and identity from their jobs than others. For the rest, work is a means to funding fulfillment in other parts of their lives. A shortage of

Table 4.1 Seven Economic Identities

Wealth	Identity	Defining Characteristics	Defining Need
Top 1%	Players	The top 1% has made it. They are world travelers, active or retired professionals, investors, and people who are generally held in high esteem. Some might also be gangster rappers.	Toys Adventures New conquests The finest things
Top 10%	Climbers	Typically, they are in the top 5% of the income distribution, or will be. Household income is in the $160K range. These are professionals who generally find meaning in their jobs and expect that education and hard work will earn them a comfortable professional and personal life. They are not looking to change the system, just master it as it is.	Stability and planning Simplification Upward mobility Networking Affordable luxury
	Libertines	This group might earn as much as Climbers, but can have the widest income range because their pursuits can be varied. Many fall into the 36% surveyed by MetLife in 2011 who said they want to quit their jobs in the next 12 months. Many will pursue their entrepreneurial, social, or artistic passions. America's micropreneurs will come from this group.	Tools and services for entrepreneurial empowerment Know-how Networking Access to capital Purpose
Top 40%	Toilers	Most people earning $35,000–$80,000 a year will fall into this category. They see work as a way to support their families and meet financial obligations. Many watch helplessly as health and education costs eat away at their stagnating salaries. They crave actualization, but will likely seek and receive it outside of their work lives.	Hobbies and causes Opportunities for their kids Discounts and savings
	Bothered Boomers	Baby boomers are in the decline of their earning years. Starting January 2011 and continuing through 2020, 10,000 boomers will retire each day. Boomers are concerned about their health, their families, and making their money last.	Simpler investments Affordable health care Late-life jobs Hobbies
	Tech Turks	Young people from rich or poor families that are looking to find their way in the world. This group, whether they come from money or not, has always existed, trying to find their identity. With technology, they'll have more ways than ever to do it. The question remains, can they earn a living at it?	Digital tools Networking opportunities Opportunities to prove themselves Platforms to express skills
Bottom 50%	Subsisters	The 44 million on food stamps or any household earning less than $35,000 falls into this category. This is an increasingly disenfranchised group with debilitating un- or underemployment. Most Subsisters are not college graduates.	Something for the kids Insurance Reasons to have hope Safety Jobs

higher paying jobs, an unbalanced education system, and good old-fashioned aging produced several high-skilled labor pools that will supply virtually free labor for companies that can offer something worthwhile in return.

Write Stuff

One abundant, underemployed group consists of writers and journalists. When the Internet turned everyone into a writer, the sheer volume of content drove down everyone's value. Colleges haven't stopped churning out new content producers, but consumers are maxed out. Going forward, most new content will have to steal audience from other sources. Consequently, wages for writers will continue to fall—sometimes below zero. Some are already monetizing this surplus. Groupon employs a swarm of writers to spice up its deal postings. It's a little trick they borrowed from Woot!, an older deals site. Squidoo, Flixya, Examiner, and HubPages have writers contribute in exchange for a share of their articles' ad revenues. The resulting income ranges between homelessness and poverty.

Writers are encouraged to actively promote their articles, but mostly the platform benefits. (It's similar to class action lawsuits where the law firm gets the big money and each plaintiff gets a $40 check.) Yahoo! bought several of these content farms in order to get money from page views. Of course the granddaddy of them all is Huffington Post, which was sold to AOL for $315 million. A majority of the site's content consists of commentary on other people's articles (at places like the *Wall Street Journal* and the *New York Times*). Its posts are usually written by a network of unpaid bloggers.

Auditioning 2.0

It's clear employers have the leverage in a weak market. Many can even get free work done through their recruiting activities by asking recruits to prove they can do it first. GILD by Pac Labs offers a platform where tech job candidates compete in employer-sponsored challenges. Those who deliver the best work, get jobs.

Candidates also compete to get certified in various levels of Oracle, Microsoft, and HP technologies, which, incidentally, creates a big revenue stream. Informally, others are doing the same. A day after Google unveiled Instant, its new search technology that displays results as you type, an independent developer created a similar, unauthorized version for YouTube. The head of YouTube tweeted him a job offer the next day, telling him he could quit school. More and more companies can see proof of work before hiring, whether it is through competitions or structured environments.

Older Workers

The population of Bothered Boomers is growing by 10,000 a day and Social Security teeters on a political and financial cliff. Most seniors aren't financially, physically, or psychologically ready to quit working. They'll be even less so when the government raises the retirement age, forcing many to stay in the workforce. Luckily, many seniors are smarter, more dependable, and willing to work for less than younger counterparts because they're supplementing a pension or other retirement income. That means they'll also require fewer benefits. Plus, older workers have lower turnover.

On average, turnover costs companies $2,300 in recruiting, training, and lost productivity. During the housing boom, Home Depot employed older workers who worked in construction, carpentry, or related fields. Borders books used to hire retired teachers and librarians. At one point, 16 percent of the company's employees were 50 or older. In the next decade, older workers can help provide a steady hand in turbulent times. They may not be looking to change the world, but like any form of diversity, they can bring experience and discipline to situations that might unnerve or annoy digitally distracted younger workers.

Unwitting Laborers

One of the most brilliant deployments of free labor was made possible by modern technology. Google and other firms that have been scanning and digitizing millions of books, documents, and articles developed a brilliant ploy. You know those CAPTCHAS that present you with those squiggly, mangled words for you to decipher to prove you're human when buying concert tickets? Usually, only one of the two words is the real security word. The other is a word from a scanned document that couldn't be recognized. You are working for free to decipher it. When I say you, I mean millions of people deciphering words that help digitize millions of publications. It's brilliant and possible to do in other ways. In the 1990s and early 2000s, screensavers that used your computer's idle processing time were popular. These screensavers created a network of users to compute complex scientific equations that would otherwise have required a massive supercomputer or a benevolent alien.

Open Sourcerers

There has been a huge movement among programmers to liberate software from corporations and make it free. Many have put their time where their mouths are. Mozilla's Firefox (and other programs) are all built by groups of collaborating programmers. Linux, an operating system that threatened to take shares from Microsoft, was also built by volunteers. Wikipedia attracts a similar, though somewhat less technical, crowd of volunteers.

This pool of revolutionaries is hard, but not impossible, to tap. Companies that want software or to build an ecosystem of developers (which many should be considering) could use open source projects as a way to build goodwill with the developer community. The best example was Google's Android mobile operating system. The platform was open sourced, so developers could add and improve code, while hardware manufacturers could install it license-free. These same developers became passionate about Google and Android in ways that they weren't around Apple's iOS or BlackBerry's platforms. In a way, it's a freemium model. You make something open source but can monetize other relationships and related services around the platform.

College Internships

Eager, wide-eyed college kids have provided a steady stream of free labor for decades. While professions such as finance always paid interns, industries like media and entertainment never had to. When the recession hit, unpaid internships shot through the roof and colleges were deluged with requests. As paid workers were laid off, this was the next best thing. At some point, unpaid interns practically got their own interns. A *New York Times* piece criticized unpaid internships as glorified slavery since the programs implicitly favor rich kids who can afford to not work for a summer.

There are better ways to structure internships, like linking them to objective performance measures, job interviews, and future employment opportunities. To avoid the perception of unfairness, companies may also want to consider offering corporate housing to less well-off interns; financial aid offices at schools could at the very least, take on the paperwork needed to hold companies to their promises.

Effortless Volunteerism

When people do things they don't like for free, they feel enslaved. When they volunteer for charity they feel empowered. And when they get paid to do what they would do for free, they are self-actualized. Since the recession, volunteerism is on the rise, but the more interesting angle is combining volunteerism with a fair financial benefit to all parties. There are many models like that emerging.

My friend and former colleague Tania Mulry might be on to something unique in marrying those two worlds. She recently started edRover to raise money for schools. When someone with an edRover phone app checks in or buys something at a local merchant, that merchant donates money to the customer's school of choice. It's an elegantly balanced, systematic model that eliminates the usual begging and discomfort of charity fundraising. Goodsearch does something similar. It wants you to use its search engine. Your reward for defying the all-powerful Google is donations to your school for clicks and purchases. In both cases, you're getting paid to volunteer, and no one feels bad about it.

Another example of meaningful commerce is microlending. Originally conceived as an interest-free way to lend small amounts of money to people in the emerging world, the segment became a business. While some organizations, like Kiva, still operate as non-profits, others are unabashedly capitalist. In and of itself, that is not a bad thing. When SKS Microfinance Ltd, India's largest micro-lender went public, shares surged. The company also attracted prominent investors like George Soros and Infosys founder N.R. Narayana Murthy. The reality is, within reason, a well-run, well-capitalized private enterprise can reach more people, manage expenses better, and self-sustain—all while helping more people.

What Minimum Wage? Tiny Jobs for Tiny Pay

While not everyone will work for free, many are getting awfully close. The two greatest changes sweeping the U.S. labor force are continued impermanence and micronization of jobs. Even the definition of what is a job is in question. Some companies are starting to adapt to these new roles and their shrinking salaries. In fact, they're not even salaries. This gets around the minimum wage debate altogether by using fixed prices for projects and tasks, instead of hourly wages. Even if it takes someone 10 hours to do a $50 project, the onus is on the individual, not the employer. This might be the way employment works in the near future.

From Jobs to Projects

Services like Sologig.com, Elance, and Guru.com have made it easier than ever for employers to chop up a job and post it as a series of projects. Elance alone has about 700,000 freelancers. These sites charge membership fees based on volume or commissions by project of up to 9 percent. A surprising range of jobs can be sourced this way—from business strategy to web development to graphics design. The ease of getting smart, global employees in short, manageable bursts is probably the greatest boon for employers and threat for domestic knowledge workers.

From the employer's point of view, there are chunks of entire departments that can be "projectized" or exported. The advantage of a full-time, domestic employee is cultural and contextual. A web design or strategy is one thing, but adapting it to local behaviors and each company's nuances is another matter. On freelancer sites, each provider's reviews and reputation scores will reflect how well they deliver on these intangibles. We are moving to a future where everyone's project rating, reputation score, and ID will be portable across networks and evolve over an entire lifetime. Of course, older ratings would get de-emphasized in the system over time. LinkedIn and Monster.com, for example, are well positioned to do this.

From Projects to Microtasks

Just when you thought projects were small, task-based labor has arrived. And some of it is barely recognizable as work. People sign up to do tasks at places like CrowdFlower, which pays people Swag Bucks to do things like review a resume, provide financial consulting, or post positive reviews of a business on Yelp or Twitter. It could take as many as seven hours of work to earn enough Swag Bucks for a $5 Amazon gift certificate.

Possibly inspired by the "What would you do for a Klondike Bar?" commercial, Fiverr.com skips the virtual currency altogether. It lets its 60,000 buyers and sellers decide what each party is willing to do for $5. This ranges from planning trips to providing wake-up calls to fitness counseling. Amazon has one of the most successful operations in this Tech Turk genre. It processes hundreds of thousands of Human Intelligence Tasks (HITs) with a rated, categorized, 24 × 7 workforce that client companies can deploy at will.

Either the race to the bottom has begun or this is the very last phase of outsourcing. Domestically, this type of model attracts Toilers or bored Tech Turks looking for a few extra bucks or to satisfy a gaming fix. In emerging markets, $5 can be a lot of money. These may be real jobs for some, creating economic incentive to learn English or pay for Internet. Facebook is also getting into the menial demi-jobs space by paying people pennies to watch ads. People earn credits that can be redeemed for Facebook deals.

Extending the Tiny Pay Model

Employers are saving big money by applying this same psychological pricing to incentivize employees. BetterWorks, at $4 per employee per month, offers perks through employers. Mainly, they are discounts on everyday spend items like gyms, laundry, and salons. Pricelock offers a different twist. It enables companies to offer employees gas discounts. The Miles of Smiles program at Aegis gave call center employees a $.50 per gallon discount, but only cost $15 per employee per month. Miles of Smiles had a 99 percent participation rate and reduced attrition by up to 50 percent. In call centers, reducing turnover saves as much as $2,000 per person in recruiting and training costs.

Even major financial services companies are implementing points systems. One credit card company's program creates a points budget at each business unit that can be used to reward excellence. Points are redeemed for gift cards or merchandise, just like credit card points. It's a powerful psychological tool. Once someone has a big enough balance, they become vested in the points system. Travel rewards are a classic example of this. Some get so obsessed that they'll book random flights to anywhere during the Christmas holidays just to retain their Elite status. That luggage-less vagrant sitting next to you in first class is no terrorist, it's a Plutonium Lounge member with a little too much time on his hands.

Everyone's a Business

With jobs shrinking and pay stagnating, people (Toilers in particular) will look for other ways to make money. Several models are emerging that do just that. Many focus on monetizing idle assets. Getaround allows people to make money by letting others rent their car when it's not being used. The company provides an easy-to-install door opener that is remotely activated through a renter's iPhone. The company also provides insurance coverage for both parties. Other companies are offering the same rental model for idle apartments, houses, and offices. AirBnB turns any apartment in the world into a Bed and Breakfast. Not only that, it raised $112 million in venture capital to do it. Billguard rewards people for reviewing your bills. SkillShare makes everyone into a paid teacher. Several other start-ups are in the works that allow people to easily sell or recycle their unused possessions.

Social Identity as Economic Leverage

In a way, social tools are a counterbalance to the increasing power of corporations. In the past, people were defined by their trades— fisherman, farmer, Samurai, and so forth. Technology has allowed people to have individuality outside of their profession. It's similar to the way a phone now represents a person instead of a place. In the future, all identities will be social, digital, and portable. They'll also be public. That gives individuals unprecedented economic leverage as consumers and employees. Companies must understand and embrace that new level of empowerment.

Consumer Leverage

I recently ordered a laptop from a well known Chinese manufacturer. To protect the guilty, let's call them LemonPC. When it arrived, I didn't like the design; plus the huge power supply made the entire rig less than portable. I tried calling the company's customer service numbers and no one picked up. I accessed their online chat and was mysteriously disconnected when I questioned their 15 percent restocking fee. I was mad and out of options, except maybe disputing the charge on my Amex card. Instead, I decided to tweet about it. This is what I wrote:

> @ideafaktory: NEVER BUY A @LEMONPC computer! They don't answer calls, disconnect your chats, demand a 15% restocking fee & adapter is bigger than a brick!!

In less than 10 minutes, I received a tweet back from LemonPC apologizing and offering to fix the situation. Among those tweets, one exchange in particular exemplifies exactly how powerful consumers have become:

> @lemonpc: Thank you. Outside of the restocking fee, is there anything else you are dissatisfied with? The RS fee is a company policy.
>
> @ideafaktory: Every company has policies that might result in dissatisfied customers blogging & tweeting until 1000 people stop buying your products.

Within two hours I got two calls from LemonPC's India call center offering a full refund and free return shipping.

Twitter, Facebook, blogging, and web sites like Consumerist.com empower people who were quickly losing leverage. The ability to impact bottom lines through influence will create new levels of corporate accountability and responsiveness. Companies like Klout are beginning to identify who these influencers are and how much social firepower they are packing. More importantly, the success of Libertines and Tech Turks will attract some Climbers and Toilers into the fold. That shift will occasionally snowball into deeper demands of corporations—everything from more domestic production to green standards to concessions on wages. Even Boomers, who see this power shift happening, will start to use social media to demand benefits and better service. More likely, interest groups will do some of it on their behalf.

One such power broker is a start-up looking to replace the court system with the threat of public shaming. PeopleClaim charges consumers $7.95 per complaint filing. If the complaint isn't resolved by the company within a period specified by the consumer (between two weeks and 90 days), the claim is posted publicly on the site for all to see. The company charges extra to file formal complaints with regulatory agencies. Though it's still in the early stages, PeopleClaim provides what many without blogs or social media empires need, for a very small investment. Of course shame only works if people can see it, so the site's ability to weave itself into the social ecosystem will determine its success. There is more opportunity lurking in these explicit, shame-based models.

Career Leverage

There's the reputation people have at work, and now, the one they have in the public eye. Not only is everyone a star, everyone is a public figure and a brand. The importance of building and maintaining that brand is already creating services like Reputation. com that help people and companies manage their online brands— from search results to tweets to reviews on Yelp. Everyone is open to scrutiny. Once you've managed the risk, the rest is about establishing a substantive reputation.

The same way most adults only post their best pictures on Facebook, they will also create online identities geared to maximize their marketability. It's clear where this is headed. The more credibility someone establishes outside their employment, the more leverage that person has in negotiating with their employer on salary, promotions, or if they're fired. Just like online influence can get you a quick refund on a laptop, it will also make the more effective communicators, like Libertines and Tech Turks, freestanding entities who command respect from employers simply because they have influence. Even the influence of the less rambunctious Toilers and image-conscious Climbers can no longer be discounted.

Scoring Fame and Esteem

A 2008 survey conducted in Britain asked 2,500 people ages 16 to 21 what they wanted to be. Just over half said they wanted to be music or TV stars and 14 percent wanted to be "celebrities" . . . completely bypassing the talent portion of the competition. (As for the rest, 13 percent wanted to be teachers, 11 percent lawyers and 8 percent nurses.) The message is that Tech Turks will use social celebrity as a means of building esteem. Platforms like Foursquare and games from companies like Zynga create a fun, superficial way of rewarding "success." I'm not sure what powers the Mayor of Milkshake Shack has, but I'm sure it was a lot easier to get than a nursing degree. For many, the same gaming and esteem logic applies to the number of friends or followers they have on various social networks. After all, it's just another score.

For some, the number of friends they have on Facebook or followers on Twitter is a sign of validation and a payment of sort. Still, like Foursquare, the reward is disconnected from any true meaning to people. One site that's getting this right is Seeking Alpha. This financial site generates expert-driven content. Typically, financial advisors or economists write articles for the site. They get compensated in the same way Twitter users do—with followers. Yet, there is a fundamentally different flavor to this popular site because followership on Seeking Alpha could generate new clients, career advancement, or validation of your way of thinking. For now, it's the gold standard for systems that sell actualization without actually paying a wage.

Up to a point, companies can use this logic in designing their customer and reward systems, more of which can now be based on fame, not cash. Creating an effective fame-based currency is no easy task for most companies. Big brands with passionate customers, chunky marketing budgets, and lots of web traffic could do it. Even they might find it easier to partner with or buy existing fame-based currencies that have shown widespread adoption by the company's target demographic. Partnering with Foursquare or using another check-in API will still cost less than rebates, bonuses, and other cash incentives. Because these may only motivate Tech Turks, Libertines, and Toilers (for very different reasons), esteem-based currencies should be a complementary part of an incentive portfolio, not its bread and butter.

Secure Future

Boomers attain actualization by watching their kids and grandkids succeed while enjoying a secure retirement. According to Nielsen, 51 percent of them will not be able to maintain their living standards. The other 49 percent might be in better financial shape, but their psychology is equally uncertain. Toilers, Climbers, and Subsisters are no less worried, but they have time to earn their way to financial security.

Life Planning

Financial planning needs to be reinvented. Not only were pre-retirees heavily invested in stocks before the recession, but they were sold products neither they nor the brokers understood. Much was based on narrow models and assumptions and not well aligned with their goals, health, or family situations. Personal financial planning needs to evolve beyond investments and taxes. It needs to include career, health care, and education planning. For example, it might recommend expat work in countries with lower tax rates and cheaper education.

This does not have to be just for the affluent. Automated, online versions of this can help. Companies like Betterment are already simplifying investment portfolios, while Career Cubicle helps people track their careers, set goals, and plan. Many financial sites help plan for education savings, but it's usually as a separate enterprise. Bringing some of these concepts together into a smart life plan is a big step toward real security.

Savings

As boomers retire, they'll have more leisure time than ever, but limited incomes with which to enjoy it. In-home entertainment and cooking will become a viable alternative for travel and dining out. Movies, TV, and casual and social gaming will be popular. I envision lots of iPad chess, mahjong smackdowns, and travel-themed Wii games. Simplified social networking tools like Skype, Facebook, and online dating will be popular as will Kindles or other reading devices. Local events will experience a resurgence as rising fuel costs make foreign travel too pricey for most. Wal-Mart called this trend "cocooning," and stocked its stores with items to help consumers turn their homes into woodsy lodges complete with barbecues, outdoor games, and woodland critters.

One model companies could take advantage of is front-loaded pricing. As retiree incomes decline, necessities could actually become cheaper. Boost Mobile, a prepaid subsidiary of Sprint, did just that, albeit for a very different reason. Boost created a pricing plan with Shrinkage that lowers monthly fees by $5 every six months if the customer pays on time. The $50 unlimited plan drops to $35 for the last 6 months and pricing resets after two years. Similar principles can be applied to senior pricing for everything from summer rentals to Internet service to car payments.

So What?

This chapter was all about tapping into people's core need to actualize. Of course, digital tools and motivational models can only take you so far. It's a little like fortifying a Twinkie with vitamins and minerals—better for you, but it's still not quite a carrot. A deeper, more fundamental type of fulfillment bubbles beneath the surface of this new esteem model. It's one based on making real things and attracting foreign capital along the way. In the next chapter, I talk about specific ways companies can take advantage of our transition from Twinkies to carrots.

CHAPTER 5

Build a Capital Magnet

A wimpy dollar isn't enough to get Gwyneth Paltrow to work the assembly line at an Iowa Toyota plant. When combined with domestic stagnation and emerging market growth, it may just be enough to spark making things that attract foreign capital. Only production and the resulting constellation of jobs can help domestic businesses and an indebted nation grow. It's not just about creating jobs, it's about jobs that create. This is one of those rare times that the interests of business, government, and individuals align perfectly. Building a capital magnet isn't strictly about manufacturing. It's about doing the kinds of things that bring in money from places that have money.

There are three ways to become a capital magnet:

1. **Making things we can export.** Russians, Chinese, and others can copy our Lady Gaga, Facebook, and Cialis formula, but high-end physical goods are much harder to copy. There are some emerging areas of opportunity the United States has to seize. Ironically, many of the best ones will focus on helping emerging markets grow, like biotech and green energy.
2. **Replacing (or repelling) imports and cutting existing costs.** Oil is our biggest import, but there are many others. To keep U.S. money circulating here, companies will be incentivized to create new ecosystems built around domestically produced goods.
3. **Attracting foreign capital.** Our products don't have to go there as long as their money comes here. We have some incredible assets that can make this possible.

The government realizes the importance of capital magnetism. That is why President Obama appointed GE's CEO Jeff Immelt to help drive a resurgence in production and exports. We're already seeing a fleeting historical glitch that bucks the trend of automation and digitization. Since 2010, one of every six jobs created in the U.S. was in manufacturing. Companies like Ford, General Motors, Caterpillar, and Otis Elevator have all been hiring in the low thousands. If U.S. businesses can get this right, we'll never again have to see a U.S. president or American executive beg China to let our web sites and banks compete in their market.

So how will this happen?

Sell to China, India, and Brazil

The best kind of export is one that has pull. No one had to tell wealthy Chinese or Indians about iPhones and Mercedes. Customers line up for good products. U.S. companies know they can't afford to stay out of those markets and the U.S. government knows it can't create jobs if U.S. firms are unsuccessful. Some like Procter & Gamble flourished abroad, while others, including the mighty Wal-Mart, struggle. Challenges range from strict regulations to unreliable partners, to flat out favoritism of domestic competitors. Some Chinese manufacturers even plant bugs in offices of Western partners to steal trade secrets. There are conspiracy theories about spyware built into Chinese-made laptops. I'm sure Oliver Stone is writing a movie about it right now. The paranoia is understandable— many of the country's biggest companies are directly or indirectly state-controlled. Of course, that could never happen here in Americ—oh wait, Citi, Ford, and AIG. Well, we do it with such style and grace.

Build to Spec in China

In some ways, modern China is like a cross between the Renaissance and Armageddon. Commerce is thriving; everything is modernizing and bustling with activity. Yet, people are piled on top of each other and toil away in conditions straight out of a Dickens novel, minus the glamour. Imagine 1.4 billion people going through the Industrial Revolution, dot-com boom, Perestroika, and Civil Rights movement at the same exact time. Welcome to China. The next decade, like the one before, will be tumultuous, productive, and bittersweet. Some Chinese will be able to stop and smell the roses, while others could lose a finger if they stop for any reason.

Consumer Goods   In this Wild West of commerce, there are plenty of unmet needs and a formula for winning innovations:

- **Long-term security.** Chinese, on average, save more than 50 percent of their income. They'll need every penny. Pensions are pure science fiction, unless you work for the government. In most cases, if you coast into retirement with all 10 fingers, you've made it.
- **Products that last.** Chinese customers buy for value not just price. They'll save for a decade, sleeping on lumps of cash. Then one day, they'll bring a satchel of bills to a store and buy the best mattress they can afford. And it better last. The same goes for fashion. No trendy dresses you can wear only once. You better be able to get married *and* swim in it.
- **Show it off.** China alone has a million millionaires while millions of others join the middle class each year. What good is striking it rich if you can't brag a little? Most Chinese won't get a grill of gold teeth or chrome-plate everything they own. They will buy items that advertise their status—clothes, cell phones, perfumes, cuddly nonedible pets. The luxury market is growing at 20 percent a year and will soon be the largest in the world.
- **Foreign = good.** A McKinsey survey showed 52 percent of Chinese earning over $37,000 per year preferred foreign brands to domestic ones.*
- **Anything for Junior.** When you're only allowed one child, that's a lot of eggs in one basket. There's nothing two parents and four grandparents wouldn't buy for the little one . . . as long as it's educational and guarantees future success. Send your stinkin' dolls and G.I. Tsos to some other country. This pattern of behavior even has a name: "Little Emperor Syndrome."

---

*www.mckinsey.com/locations/greaterchina/mckonchina/reports/mcKinsey_wealthy_consumer_report.pdf.

- **For boys only.** Finally, China is, pardon the technical term, a sausagefest. There are 120 men for every 100 women. That's 32 million more boys than girls. Abortions of female fetuses are disturbingly high. That creates a ripple effect in everything from jobs to entertainment to security. This decade we'll see what happens when 32 million lustful, angry young men find out there's no one to date. I'm not sure if testosterone can flip over a tank, but we're about to find out.
- **Shrink it down.** Over the past two decades, P&G and Unilever realized people in India couldn't afford Costco-sized bottles of shampoo. Instead, they made a fortune selling affordable, single-use packets of many products. Tata Group, which launched the Nano, a $2,200 basic car for the Indian market, did the same for hotels. Tata's fast-growing Ginger chain provides middle class locals and business people affordable luxury at about $40 a night. The secret: reducing lobby sizes, automating many services, and eliminating multiple restaurants.

Anything produced here would have to be defensible in the Chinese market. That means highly efficient, specialized production that would be difficult to mimic or reverse-engineer. Intel's chip architecture falls into this category. Even the Chinese want a Boeing 767, not a Shengzhou 321. It doesn't have to be a megacorporation. TurboFil, a 10-person company from New York state, successfully exports cosmetics packaging and filling machines to Sri Lanka, Peru, Guatemala, and other countries.

Infrastructure Challenges   Emerging markets will invest well over $10 trillion in infrastructure over the next decade. U.S. firms can help China, Mexico, India, and Brazil with fuel generation, sewage and water systems, logistics for transporting people and goods, and more reliable crop yields and food supplies. (The Chinese definition of food is slightly broader than ours. It includes turtles, snouts, and exotic lizards.) Urban sprawl alone will create plenty of opportunity. China is planning several megacities that range from 50 million to 260 million residents. (Something it wouldn't need if it eliminated its draconian internal passport system.)

In the United States, pollution is a byproduct of consumption. In China it's a byproduct of necessity. Here, a Prius is something a sitcom actor drives as a badge of pride. Abroad, a factory making parts for that Prius needs somewhere to dump its waste. It's hard to be too judgmental when someone else is doing all your dirty work. Urban pollution kills 300,000 Chinese citizens each year. That is a very real green challenge U.S. companies could help solve.

China walks a fine line when managing the possibility of social unrest. So many people are so poor that inflation could lead to revolution. That is why the country subsidizes the poor and enforces a strict, but tiny minimum wage.

Deconstructing Success Stories

Some foreign companies are not only showing what it takes to succeed in emerging markets, they're hinting at big, unmet needs where U.S. companies can play. The following are just a few of those examples.

Customization and Tradition   dENiZEN Jeans makes slimmer fits, Hermès uses traditional Chinese art in its designs, and BMW released an M3 Tiger to coincide with the Chinese New Year. Even Apple employees wear T-shirts that say, "Designed in California, Made for China." Incidentally, I wore the same exact slogan to an Asian singles' event many years ago. It did not go well.

Cheaper Models   Tata started the trend of ultracheap cars you don't have to push, like my dad's Soviet-made Fiat in the 1970s. Now, Honda, Nissan, and GM make stripped down cars for China that balance local preferences with local budgets, typically under $5,000. At that price, the United States might only produce a very slow moving sofa.

Pay As You Go   Cell phone companies have done it for years. Now companies across the business spectrum are letting people pay for things in installments. Microsoft successfully sold PCs in China that way.

Solve a Problem   In eight months, Tough Stuff sold 200,000 solar power units to poor families that can now power lamps, phones, and radios with clean, free energy. International Development Enterprises (India) sells irrigation equipment to farmers. For less than $40, they can grow crops year round. So much for that *Judge Judy* marathon during dry season.

Repurpose and Reuse   Several companies, like Husk Power Systems, have come up with a way to create mini power plants using abundant, inedible cornhusks as fuel. Personally, I can't wait until there's a way to power my home using banished *American Idol* contestants.

Simple, Mobile   SoukTel created a text message-based employment service in the Middle East. (I think it's how Qaddafi got his job.) The BBC uses audio and SMS to teach English in Bangladesh. It also negotiated a 75 percent discount with the mobile provider. Many providers in Africa have eliminated the need for bank branches as even the simplest phone allows for cash transfers and deposits through SMS.

If You Can, Make It Here . . .

While some innovative companies like Qualcomm have abandoned manufacturing entirely, others like Caterpillar, Ford, and General Electric plan to produce more in the United States. Intel, alone, is spending more than $10 billion on new plants in Arizona, New Mexico, and Oregon. Companies like Whirlpool are looking to replace old machines and choosing to keep production here. Rising labor costs in China and Mexico, plus the distance from U.S. customers are two of the reasons. Another is that machines don't (yet) demand raises, vacations, or validation. In the long run, that's more sustainable at least until the robots self-actualize. If they do, each new Terminator might have an advanced battery from Dow Kokam or GM. Both companies plan new battery factories in the United States. It's not hard to imagine cars, homes, lawnmowers, earthmoving equipment, and mobile devices also using them.

Innovation Snowball Effect   Economists project that the next five years will see over 300,000 high-paying manufacturing jobs created in the United States. (Yes, the same economists who did not see the housing bubble.) I believe rising demand abroad, higher fuel prices, and a weaker U.S. currency can get that number to 1.5 million or more over the next decade. That's not including the digital communities, technologies, and professional services built around them. That halo effect will extend to peripheral jobs, too. After all, who wouldn't want a Tito's Taco truck on their job site or Sally's Salon to soften your gruff, engineering exterior? Maybe these days, it's more likely to be a Starbucks and a Supercuts.

Rejected by China   Only lots of small companies can deliver big numbers in manufacturing. The low hanging fruit is bringing high-end production back to the United States for existing products. Luckily, China is doing that for us. Small companies like Sleek Audio, which used Chinese partners to make its high-end headphones, are bringing production back to the U.S. The company found that quality was inconsistent, goods took forever to get here, and workers were getting expensive. Sleek Audio, like others, found itself a low priority. Big customers got the A-Team, while it was stuck with a Rube Goldberg machine run by Mao, Larry, and Curly.

Most small companies find it backbreaking to keep going back to China to fix quality issues. Adding insult to injury, Peerless Industries found knockoffs of its flat screen TV mounts competing with its own merchandise because of dodgy subcontractors. Even Nike found an entire factory down the street from its own stamping out Nike knockoffs. In 2010, consulting firm Grant Thornton found that 44 percent of smaller businesses got no benefit from outsourcing, and 7 percent believe it caused them harm.

Reverse Outsourcing   At some point, half my team at American Express was Indian. As a people, you'll find most Indians to be smart, good-natured, and hardworking. Of course, I don't have to tell you that. If you work in almost any professional field from medicine to finance, you probably know plenty of people named Patel or Shah. At the very least, you strongly suspect that the guy on the phone trouble-shooting your router isn't really named Bob. Like manufacturing, some services are ripe for a return to the U.S. shores.

The United States accounts for 63 percent of India's outsourcing revenues. Indian labor is one of the U.S.'s biggest imports. And it's not just call centers. U.S. companies have moved finance, medical scanning, software development, legal, and back-office administration there. For a while, it seemed that gifted East Indians would eventually take every job from firefighter to senator. That is until inflation caught up. Wages in India grew 11.7 percent in 2010 and 12.9 percent in 2011. Recruiting in India became excruciating.

Candidates had servants, gold bars, and fresh lamb thrown at them. Over the next few years, their cost advantage will disappear.

Ironically, Aegis, the outsourcing unit of an Indian conglomerate, is leading the way in bringing call center jobs back to the U.S. It's now "near-sourcing," or putting support closer to customers. Companies like American Express and Humana prefer support done in the United States. Companies with sensitive data wisely prefer to keep customers' dirty little secrets from crossing borders. Aegis had 5,000 U.S. employees in 2011 with plans to triple that number. Tata, another Indian conglomerate, also plans to near-source. Genpact is buying back-office operations from Walgreens and providing those services domestically for less.

You probably know all the old jokes about lawyers. For years, they were everywhere and law schools popped up like Subway franchises. Ambulance chasing and legal fees threatened to consume the United States from the inside, like Ebola. Finally, companies had had enough. As schools continued to churn out bushels of lawyers, companies negotiated fixed-fee deals and outsourced many administrative and basic legal functions to places like India. Suddenly, India had American law schools. Recently, companies like Pangea3 and Integreon, which led the international outsourcing parade, started bringing jobs back to the United States, hiring American lawyers for $50,000 to $80,000, instead of the more than $100,000 they used to earn. Though lawyers don't get the camaraderie, mentoring, and free pretzels of traditional law jobs, they do get jobs. Now that employing Americans in places like North Dakota and Texas is competitive with Bangalore, there is opportunity to bring back other professions like tech and finance. We are that much closer to my dream of Indians complaining about our accents on phone support calls.

"Here Commerce"   Some people are so conscious about where their fish comes from, they practically want to interview their salmon. "Were you raised on a farm? Are you endangered? Did you come from a broken home?" After this bad date, they want the fish killed gently, with boredom, by reading it Nietzsche in its native German. A similar phenomenon is occurring with the local food movement and energy independence. In many ways, the groundwork has been laid for people to care about where products were made. This may not happen for very price sensitive consumers, but all else being equal, more people are prepared to buy domestic and pay a slight premium if it means long-term sustainability. Recession is a good teacher.

The first wave of companies that can take advantage are retailers. Maybe they can learn something from Mark Andol. The *New York Post* recently featured an article about Mark, a 47-year-old retired welder who got fed up watching friends and family lose jobs. So he opened a store in upstate New York that sells 3,000 products made entirely in the United States. Everything from molasses to paper products to hardware has its rightful, eclectic place. On opening day, he was greeted by 800 customers. "Everyone was shaking my hand and crying," Andol said. "People lost trust in the system. This gives them hope." Mark plans to open several new locations and double the number of items he carries. He also meticulously certifies that every screw of every product was indeed made in the United States.

Similarly, Wal-Mart can do for domestic production what it did for energy efficiency when it phased out incandescent bulbs. It could even have a "Made in the USA" store-within-a-store in some categories. Others like Home Depot, Best Buy, and Amazon can capitalize by promoting or rating products based on percentage made here. If McDonald's shows salt and cholesterol content in food, why couldn't "Made in . . . " labels evolve, too? Showing the macroeconomic price you pay for each TV or PC can help consumers make choices that drive favorable economics.

A second wave will come when domestic producers have something to brag about. If this trend takes off, Panasonic, Samsung, and others might just be lured to produce some of their wares domestically. It would be a bold move for companies to promote the shift. In the long run, it's one that can ensure customers have the kinds of jobs that will help them afford those products in the future.

Rise of Localism   To promote local trade, the town of North Fork, California, created its own currency. Unlike monopoly money or something creepily retrieved from Bob Barker's pants on *The Price Is Right*, North Fork Shares are legal tender and accepted at most local businesses. Ithaca Hours in Ithaca, New York, BerkShares in Massachusetts, and Plenty in Pittsboro, North Carolina, are similar currencies. The concept is simple: If you have a wallet full of these, you will use them. Game companies, Facebook, merchant gift cards, and Disney theme parks use the same logic. Are you going to leave

Disney World with a pocket full of Disney Dollars or a pair of kids strung out on Mickey's cotton candy? This could be an opportunity for card companies to facilitate local commerce and reward domestically produced goods.

Northeast Ohio created a loyalty card and online local deal exchange. In a short period of time, about 11,000 cards were sold at $10 apiece. Dan Roman, the director of the Council of Smaller Enterprises said, "Independent studies have found 68 cents of each dollar stays in the community." That's 50 percent more than the 43-cent average for the region. Local incentive programs could be run better by companies like Amazon, Groupon, or any web company that ends with "on." Going even further, Ohio Governor Ted Strickland banned using state funds for offshore companies. That will not be the end of it. The more people understand what is in their long-term interest, the more likely they are to patronize businesses aligned with it. The private sector can profit from this sentiment.

Barter   There is one other fragmented market that can stimulate domestic and local commerce. It's barter, and it's crying out for modernization. Numerous exchanges across the United States help small businesses use barter currency, instead of cash, to facilitate local deals. ITEX is among the largest, but there are hundreds of others. In Australia, BarterCard had more volume than American Express and Diners Club in 2009. Despite its success, the company has its share of negative reviews. Most of these small players still feature the kind of digital capabilities you'd expect in biblical times when three goats cost 10 chickens. Companies focused on local services like Angie's List, Groupon, or ServiceMagic are well positioned to do this at scale while capitalizing on the local commerce movement.

Local Investing   One of the most intriguing ways to stimulate investment in local businesses comes from across the pond. Investbx allows U.K. investors to buy shares in private businesses located in the West Midland region. Teamworks Karting, a go-cart center, raised $735,000 to open a new location. Tech firm Key Technologies raised $3 million on the exchange. Because I am American, I love to supersize. In this case, I'd love to see this model scale in the United States.

A good way to do it might be for financial firms to create and sell mutual funds that invest in local businesses. Their popularity would soar if, with a little lobbying, they could get these funds to be exempt from federal, state, and local taxes just like municipal bonds.

Change the Model

The most powerful but frequently overlooked forms of innovation focus on changing how a company makes money, is structured, or who its customers are. Creating new business models is probably the best way to ensure export success. It might also be the only way to make the math work in hostile, cost-driven markets.

Infrastructure with a Pinch of Communism

When it comes to manufacturing and exporting efficiently, now is the perfect time to rethink what parameters are worth competing on and which ones aren't. Shared procurement and common infrastructure are close cousins of outsourcing. For example, European mobile companies share their GSM network infrastructure but still compete on features, brand, price, customer service, and other levers. Vodafone does the same in India with its Indian competitors. In the U.S., a perverse hodgepodge of frequencies and mobile technologies duplicate efforts and confuse consumers. In payments, Visa, MasterCard, American Express, and to some extent, Discover, often use the same Independent Sales Organizations to distribute terminals compatible with all four networks. In most cases, the economics of exclusive acceptance stopped making sense. When it comes to buying from or selling to foreign markets, it might not be a bad idea to consider pooling sales, procurement, platforms, facilities, and distribution with other players in the market.

Trend Spies

Not every company can afford a big R&D budget, local surveys, and frequent trips to check on foreign factories, competing products, and potential knockoffs. For smaller firms looking to export, there is an opportunity to pool resources to put "trend spies" into every market. Like the Associated Press does in journalism, trend spies would act as a shared, syndicated function that helps identify trends, unmet needs, and new opportunities. These spies don't have to be permanent or limited to just trends.

Some can be tasked with forging domestic import/export relationships, selling products, finding and evaluating suppliers, or protecting domestic intellectual property. Consulting, logistics, and sales companies are positioned to play in this space. For now, companies can turn to the U.S. Commercial Service's international partner search that for $500 helps U.S. companies find and screen up to six Chinese partners (agents, distributors, licensees, franchisees, joint ventures, and so on). The department also offers detailed reports on partners for $600 each. Call 1-800-USA-TRADE now and you'll also get this mini salad shooter for just the cost of shipping and handling.

Connect Businesses

Another untapped opportunity is helping U.S. companies that operate in emerging markets compete there more effectively. Examples include IP protection services, factory surveillance equipment, and supplier selection and management. Procurement software company Ariba is well positioned to capitalize with its Discovery service, which matches small businesses with global corporate buyers. Everything from office cleaning to payroll and accounting services can be sold this way. Initially, the system is RFP based, but there is room for more expansive selling and true discovery of new products, services, and suppliers that can find demand overseas.

For the longest time, one company that fascinated me was China's Alibaba. It seemed to have a hand in almost every online basket. From digital payments to online marketplaces, it looked like eBay, Amazon, Ariba, and PayPal all rolled in one. The part of its business that was most interesting was its marketplace that matches Chinese manufacturers with smaller, foreign buyers. Anything from complex electronics to coffee mugs can be procured on the site. Recently, the company added services to help protect intellectual property rights. The company makes money from subscription fees to become a verified seller and from selling value-added services, like financing. Not only do U.S. companies need to tap into this powerful platform, they'll have the chance to reverse its flow. U.S. companies can become suppliers into this marketplace and develop even better ways to facilitate U.S. exports.

Multinational as Distributor

Just as "cleaner fish" remove dead skin and parasites from other fish, some multinational corporations can become the sales forces for products made by small, domestic producers. For a fee, they can use their expertise and foreign relationships to distribute a wider range of products for companies that would otherwise get eaten alive in places like China. U.S.-based small businesses could then manage one relationship *here* instead of a ledger full of political incentives there.

Lock In Capital Advantage

Most airlines use sophisticated hedging to stabilize fuel costs in case violence breaks out in the Middle East or beefy passengers stampede the airline for a bacon convention. Food manufacturers typically do the same. Farmers are on the other side of the trade making sure they lock in a minimum profit for their crops. Under normal conditions these mechanisms work well enough. Still, in the last three years, fuel, copper, silver, grains, and other foods have hopped around like coked-up bunnies. Food prices, especially, are out of control.

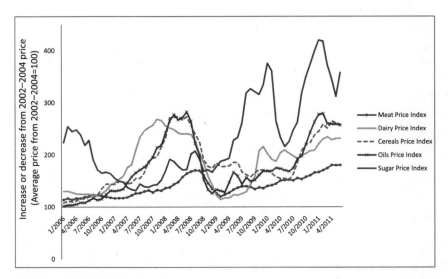

Figure 5.1   Food Prices, 2006–2011

Source: FAO Food Price Index.

There has been plenty of speculation and manipulation in silver, cocoa, and other commodities. In the 1970s, the Hunt brothers bought up 50 percent of the world's silver to drive up prices and possibly, make the world's biggest necklace. When the government changed the rules on commodities trading, their scheme collapsed. In 2008, oil speculators drove up prices for a huge profit. In 2010, investment firm Armajaro made a huge profit by buying 7 percent of the world's cocoa and selling when prices hit a 33-year high.

Those schemes are peanuts compared to what China is doing. China is unloading dollars like a plot from a bad 1980s Richard Pryor movie. Instead, it's buying something far more valuable—no, not Lady Gaga tickets—natural resources. China is on a vertical integration spree. By 2014, it will be investing over \$100 billion a year in mineral and metal mines alone. It is doing the same with other natural resources in Brazil and Venezuela. It's also colonizing Africa to mine the continent's natural resources. You thought your city had a good Chinatown . . . there are at least 750,000 Chinese settled in Africa with more on the way. Soon they'll set up local governments to help control their interests. China also has total control of 11 rare earth mines essential to high-tech manufacturing— and they've committed to reducing rare earth exports by 10 percent a year. The Chinese are playing to win.

Control means Chinese companies will get priority access to inputs at insider prices. Suddenly, every producer starts with a disadvantage even if they can get the same zinc or iron elsewhere. Not only does this situation threaten the future of domestic manufacturing, it could make us permanently dependent on China. Imagine how cranky you'd be if the same iPhone cost \$4,000 here and \$200 in Shanghai. Don't trash your wok just yet. Now is the time for companies to lock in long-term pricing for key inputs. It wouldn't be a bad idea to secure supply lines by partnering with or buying (either through consortia or directly) mines and other nonrenewable resources. Smaller domestic players, especially, could get more leverage by jointly negotiating supplier deals. Even finished goods can be procured more effectively if negotiated through a consortium.

This is no time to procrastinate on Facebook. As mentioned earlier, I believe the dollar will fall farther, so companies should sign as many long-term procurement contracts, priced in dollars, as they can. They should also borrow in dollars, but sign sales agreements in appreciating currencies whenever possible. Even companies that sell consumer staples like Campbell's or Mars should consider hedging to ride out price volatility. Now is also the time to acquire that overseas company you promised yourself for Christmas, especially if it operates in a high-growth emerging market and you plan on using cash instead of stock or mistletoe.

Hedge Everything

Price predictability isn't just for manufacturers. Not long ago, Amazon.com started offering subscriptions for foods and household products like toilet paper and shampoo. If you commit to scheduled deliveries, you can get 10 to 15 percent off. I signed up for monthly delivery of Vita Coco coconut water. A box of 12 units cost me just under $15, a 15 percent savings off the regular price. When I logged in a week later, the price had gone up by 33 percent, or $10 for my two-box order. Like most customers, I wondered if this sweet little indulgence was worth the extra cost. I could always plant a coconut tree in my apartment. If Amazon had a hedging mechanism to pre-purchase what they expect to sell, I wouldn't have this pile of sod in my living room. For two years, Amazon could have stabilized subscription prices to help customers budget and stop them from leaving because of sticker shock. A hedging mechanism for consumer goods could do that. (Ideally, it would also keep my favorite yogurt and ice cream from the supermarket shrink ray. Either I've become a giant, or my cup of La Yogurt is just a four-ounce appetizer for my next cup of La Yogurt.)

Pricelock is a relatively new company that is positioned to capitalize on this trend. It helps car fleets hedge fuel prices for up to two years. It also partnered with Hyundai to offer new customers a fixed fuel price of $1.49 per gallon for 12 months. In fact, it resulted in Hyundai being the only car company to have increasing sales after Cash for Clunkers expired and all other vehicle sales dropped like a rock. (Your government dollars hard at work.) There is room to expand this model to locking in consumer prices for food and other necessities. Even real estate companies can strike deals to lock in heating oil prices as a buyer or renter incentive.

Become a Foreign Capital Magnet

You don't have to dig a mine or build a factory to capitalize on exports. Another way is to import the foreigners themselves. No, I don't mean spending your European vacation stuffing child laborers into your Delta carry-on. Today, cash-rich visitors leave the United States with cheap souvenirs, bellies full of Olive Garden, and concussions from *Spider-Man*, the Musical. That's not enough. The United States sits on a commodity as valuable as oil, more mesmerizing than beauty, and only slightly less stable than uranium. That resource is celebrities. Our shelves are stocked with Pacinos, Gagas, and Clooneys. The U.S. needs to weaponize its creative assets in new and spectacular ways. Foreigners will have no choice but to leave a conspicuous trail of hard-earned real, yuan, and rupees all over the country. It wouldn't hurt to sell them some hair plugs and Botox treatments before they board their flights home. In fact, there are at least three categories of opportunity to attract foreign capital in bulk: entertainment, health care, and education. Each of these should be linked to incentives for future investment and entrepreneurship.

The J. Lo Hanging Fruit

If, like me, you can't tell if life is real or just a James Cameron CGI fantasy, you know how good the United States is at entertainment. Part of this success comes from our freedom and creativity. The rest can be explained by our relative wealth and leisure time. Over the last 100 years, Americans earned more, got taxed less, and had more free time than any other developed country. By the time a Cuban finishes making cigars, most Americans are home watching game shows and classic films starring Jennifer Aniston. Hollywood is a global, cultural powerhouse that can't always protect its content in countries with broadband and a crush on Angelina Jolie. Soon, the Chinese, Indians, and Brazilians will dwarf us in recreational spending. Companies with leisure assets need a way to monetize the fruits of our decadence abroad.

Duck Addiction

Disney is happy to sell you a Donald Duck DVD, but it's happier if your family becomes hopelessly addicted to visiting Disney parks and waking up in Goofy underwear. Most new bands give away their music to make new fans with the hope that those fans will eventually buy merchandise and concert tickets. That popularity might attract companies to license their music for ads, games, and movies.

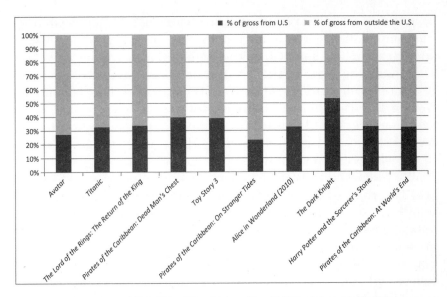

Figure 5.2 Percentage of Global Box Office Grosses (Top 10 Highest Grossing Movies)
Source: Box Office Mojo.

LiveNation, known for concert promotion, validated this shift when it signed huge talent management deals with Jay-Z, Madonna, U2, and Shakira. For the mass population, free (or nearly free) content across platforms will create fans and drive sustained cultural influence. Our cultural machine is already a juggernaut. Consider Figure 5.2. Many of our highest grossing films already make more money abroad than they do in the U.S.

Entertainment companies will make money from merchandise, theatrical releases, and live experiences in the domestic market. It's the best way to compete with popular local alternatives, like the *Dukes of Hangzhou* or *Everybody Loves Ravi*. Sports, music, movies, and theater are obvious choices to help get emerging market consumers hooked on U.S. entertainment. At the high end, this list should expand to fashion, plastic surgery, nightlife, gambling, and any other activity considered worth getting on a plane for.

Disneyfication

To build a capital magnet, rich foreigners and companies need to come here in droves—repeatedly. The way into their hearts and wallets is to think of every domestic business like a ride in a theme park. A theme park is just a bundle of good rides. If there were only one gimpy roller coaster and a hot dog cart at Disney, no one would attempt a five-hour minivan odyssey with a gang of grumpy kids. The same bundling logic applies to upscale shopping malls and cities that successfully attract visitors from remote areas. People come to New York or Paris because there is a lot to experience in one, manageable place. Wealthy visitors from the Ukraine generally miss out on the charms of Green Bay and Peoria because they lack density of attractions and potato-stuffed pierogies.

No business is an island when marketing U.S. services to foreigners. The trick is identifying anchor products or services in each bundle. In some cases, it might be a beautiful river, a landscape, or antelope-hunting season. In others, it might be a bustling art scene, great local barbecue, or a high density of top breast surgeons. Peoria may never become a destination for foreigners, but Minneapolis hotels might not be far off from offering a package that lures foreign conference organizers or fans of blues music.

Build Bundles

Identifying, packaging, and upgrading bundles of complementary services is both art and science. You wouldn't put a Chippendales show and fox-hunting excursion in the same tour package (metaphorically, perhaps). The most blatant and gaudy example of Disneyfication is Dubai. For decades, it built mind-numbing skyscrapers and wallet-munching malls, attracting wealthy visitors and investors. It even managed to get famous buyers for vacation homes on a series of man-made islands shaped like the globe. When the recession hit, many projects were halted, while others needed to refinance.

I much prefer the subtle approach South Korea's Gangnam has taken. Not known for attracting tourists, South Korea suddenly found that rich foreigners were flocking to Gangnam's 430 clinics to get plastic surgery to look like their favorite Korean celebrities. (Sadly, there were no takers for the Kim Jung Il face and hair package.) By 2015, Gangnam expects over 400,000 visitors. The clinics now have 47 envoys actively helping market their services to foreigners. The clinics are also hiring Chinese, English, and Japanese speakers to handle the volume. South Africa is also taking advantage of its abundance of cheap medical care to build surgical tourism packages. Thailand has always been a place where transgendered men go to finish the job without the mandatory multiyear counseling required in the United States. (Yes, I know, the snipped private part market won't save the economy.)

The country is brimming with international celebrities, actors, sports teams, and musicians. Creating one-of-a-kind experience packages for foreign consumers and businesses should not be that difficult. If the end of the D subway line in New York City ended with a CGI extravaganza straight out of a *Spiderman* movie, you can bet tourists would pay $35 each to experience it. They'd spend another $100 for Yankees tickets, beer, and soft pretzels. The same can work in hub-and-spoke trips. People who come to Boston for a business trip might also invite their spouses for a relaxing week on Cape Cod or a one-of-a-kind fishing trip with a Kennedy (any Kennedy will do). The same applies for tours built around sporting events, nose jobs, concerts, *American Idol* tapings, GE factory tours, Amazon.com warehouse tours, Deepak Chopra seminars, or a Britney Spears lip-syncing extravaganza.

One category ripe for development is education. In 2009, there were more than 671,000 foreign students in the U.S. getting undergraduate and graduate degrees. The Institute of International Education estimates that international students contribute about $17.6 billion to the U.S. economy with a 16 percent growth rate. Most of that growth came from China, with 62 percent of the students coming from Asia. As international college recruiters work overtime to attract foreign students, little has been done to create vacation packages for visiting parents or other word-of-mouth experiences that generate return visits by their friends and relatives. I'd also love to give every PhD grad a green card, but that's outside the scope of this book . . .

Drive Loyalty

Disneyfication wouldn't be the first time noncompeting businesses created bundles of economic activity. Nectar in the United Kingdom and Air Miles in Canada are two of the most successful multimerchant coalitions. (I created a competing one called Commerce Coalition at MasterCard.) The premise is simple—consumers earn and redeem points across multiple, noncompeting merchants using a loyalty card. Merchants share profile and shopping data to create targeted, complementary offers. For example, if you bought a grill at Home Depot, you might get a text message coupon code for steaks at a nearby Shop Rite. The same model could be adapted to foreign visitors to create loyalty packages that generate repeat visits and awareness of new experiences. Restaurants and local businesses could partner with hotels, airlines, colleges, and card companies to start building these crossborder coalitions.

Some of this could be done through social media. Using global customers' Facebook likes, custom visitor bundles can be delivered through Facebook apps like American Express' Link, Like, Love, which allows merchants to post Facebook offers that are automatically applied when a customer makes a purchase on an Amex card. This is a play on the local deals trend, but would instead deliver customized, local offers to prospective visitors.

Frictionless Marketing and Logistics

Since 9/11, I've traveled to Asia, Australia, Europe, and South America. When I wait in line at U.S. airports, sometimes I think the terrorists won. As every baby and granny is manhandled by the Transportation Security Authority, you start to wonder what it's like for foreigners visiting the country. Needless to say, that experience needs improvement, but businesses need to take all the other frictions out of the bundle experience. Whether it's transportation, dining preferences, language issues, mobile communication, or fashionable hats to cover newly transplanted hairs, the details matter. Packages and their marketing messages need to constantly evolve. In fact, there are agencies in most of those markets eager to offer something special to their customers. In the micropreneurship section, I'll talk more about how to connect with them.

What U.S. Companies Can Make in the Next Decade

Three of the biggest economic challenges facing the U.S. are about to be innovated away, just like smallpox and buying homes without incomes. These include a way to close our trade and manufacturing gap, provide affordable health care to the masses, and generate energy and jobs from thin air.

Print the Future

As a kid, I loved watching the *Jetsons*. Having seen the show as an adult, let's just say I'm grateful my kids will have cable. Two of my most vivid, geeky memories from the show are George Jetson's car that folded into a suitcase and the made-to-order food pills. Imagine the experience of wine, tapas, and small talk without the cleanup or cavities. That same level of instant gratification has taken hold in our digital lives. Every web site, game, and device contorts instantly to your tastes, dreams, and aspirations. The more life digitizes, the more our expectations for all things—digital or not—accelerate. We expect food, FedEx packages, and relationships delivered as quickly and successfully as text messages. It seems like an unwinnable battle. The real world is messy and imperfect. For those who dare to leave the house, 3-D printing is about to make the physical world worth the trip out of the house.

We're all familiar with those little ink cartridges that, at $30 for 20 milliliters, we might as well squirt Beluga caviar on a sheet of white paper. Instead of paper, there are machines that can be loaded with plastics, metals, or other raw materials to "print" three-dimensional custom molds of almost anything. The same way mobile data eliminates the time between questions and answers, 3-D printers eliminate the gap between imagination and the physical object being imagined. They started humbly enough as ways to create prototypes faster. Now, the technology is beginning to take on end to end production. Bespoke Innovations uses it to make custom, artificial limbs for $5,000 to $6,000, a tenth of what existing methods cost. Others make clothing, jewelry, fixtures, lamps, iPhone accessories, and perfume bottles. Freedom of Creation in Amsterdam used 3-D printers to make exotic furniture and fixtures for hotels and restaurants. Neri Oxman, an architect and researcher at MIT, is close to developing a machine that can build houses by printing layers of concrete.

Once you experience getting custom dress shirts from a tailor, you're unlikely to buy one off the rack with its oversized sleeves, snug collar, and conspicuous logo. Does that mean no more racks? Will The Gap stock clothes or just a body scanner, design kiosks, and a 3-D printer in the back? Everyone can have perfect jeans every time without a store employee having to restock your mounting pile of shame in that aspirational size 34. The implications and possibilities are endless. Some retailers will go from ordering finished goods to ordering cotton. From hiring sales clerks to hiring designers. From aisles full of clothes to neatly displayed samples and rows of kiosks. Stores might go from 100 employees in 5,000 square feet to 20 employees in one-fifth the space.

The technology will also spawn more entrepreneurs and businesses than ever before. It will be possible to build working prototypes that can be marketed almost instantly. One creative group of hackers in Barcelona rigged a Microsoft Kinect body motion game controller to a 3-D printer, giving tourists instant 3-D souvenirs from scans of their own bodies. New design services will help translate whatever is in your head into a design that can be shipped instantly. A company called Ponoco in New Zealand has begun putting these pieces together. It's basically a software system that sits on top of a design and manufacturing engine. They have a network of 3-D printers stationed around the world. Designers upload their designs to Ponoco and effectively "teleport" production of their object through this globally distributed manufacturing system. Even this model leaves plenty of room for automation. The killer app in this space is eliminating the barrier of design. The more easily someone can convert an idea in their head into a workable prototype image— even if they're not trained draftsmen or designers, the more entrepreneurs can be empowered to manufacture. Plenty of other business models will emerge. Soon manufacturing will be as easy as saving an appointment on Google Calendar.

If 3-D printing can scale, we'll see the end to labor in manufacturing. Machines that can easily retool and print in mass quantities will eliminate the need to import clothes, toys, and trade show knick-nacks. Immense amounts of fuel will be saved. Materials will only need to be shipped once, given the factory, distributor, and retailer might be the same entity. In the near term, U.S. companies can push the development of these machines and explore ways to use them to print increasingly complex items like electronics that can easily be moved to assembly.

This is only the beginning. Beyond this decade, there will be 3-D printers that print new 3-D printers, the same way software helps make new software. Custom food printing is next. We are not far from having a machine that can print any food using a database of recipes and techniques from the world's greatest chefs. It's not quite George Jetson's food pill, but we won't mind a little extra chewing and small talk, will we?

The Rise of Remote Health Care

I wonder if there are any people who feel a great sense of accomplishment walking out of a doctor's office. Unless something unusual gets diagnosed or you score a date with the doctor, many of the basics could have been accomplished more efficiently before your visit. With the passage of health care reform, over 30 million new people will now get coverage. Given the shortage of general practitioners and nurses, the system needs new ways to scale without taking on new labor costs and administrative overhead. Just as rice, beans, chicken, cheese, and tortillas can make up an entire Mexican menu, a range of readily available technologies can be combined in unique ways to give health care much needed scale.

The first step toward efficiency is digital records. Shockingly, all the talk has yet to produce a standard or incentive scheme worth bragging about. Each year, countless hours are wasted retrieving and inputting the same information, like *Groundhog Day* with doctors. Microsoft, Google, and others have tried solutions that failed to reach critical mass. It's going to take a consortium and new privacy standards, but it can get done. The electronics and computer industries are good examples of how to get this done. Competing manufacturers often get together to create standards with catchy acronyms like USB, Wi-Fi, HTML5, and DVD. With so much data already stored on phones and the inevitability of secure mobile wallets, smart phones will become secure hubs for storing and sharing standardized digital records, including health data.

Even without an elegant solution to the data problem, remote monitoring technology will be the next wave of health care innovation. It is the scalable killer app that will cut down on office visits and allow doctors to monitor hundreds of patients' vitals from the comfort of their iPhones. Below are a few of the technologies that are hinting at a future where visiting the doctor will be as quaint as changing channels by rolling off the couch to turn a mechanical knob on your TV:

- One of my favorites is GumPack, which was developed by a Kansas State University student. It has multiple sensors to monitor vital signs and send live data to your doctor through the Web. It also has a webcam and Wi-Fi in case you want to show off that impeccable liver.

- The Spiroscout inhaler uses GPS and Wi-Fi to track and aggregate asthma attacks, which can improve diagnoses, long-term treatment, and overall population trends.
- Under Armour's E39 performance shirt creatively combines readily available sensors and technologies to monitor athletes. It's already being used by the NFL to track heart rate, breathing, and irregular movements to optimize performance. It will not, however, allow golfers' wives to monitor irregular trips to the nightclub. This technology could eventually connect to health networks, insurers, and 911 for high-risk patients. For some, it could replace expensive Medicaid home attendants.
- GE already produces a $1,000 electrocardiogram and a $15,000 ultrasound machine in India. Home versions or ones that can be cheaply deployed in local clinics, schools, or job sites won't be far behind. The cheaper, smaller, and more self-service these machines can get, the less dependent you'll be on general practitioners who can check out any abnormal results from the golf course.
- Guardly is an ambitious app that has an initial goal of replacing 911 using smartphone location data to make emergency response more efficient. It transfers critical health data and notifies emergency contacts. In its next phase, the company plans to link glucose monitors, heart rate monitors, and other biometric devices to your phone for the kind of monitoring that can save lives and trips to the doctor.
- The name NutriSmart sounds innocent enough, except it expects you to ingest its technology. The company plants RFID chips into your food to track its entire path through your body and transmits its findings through Bluetooth to your phone. This could help the morbidly obese track calorie intake. Hospitals and doctors could use it to monitor the diets of thousands of patients on- or off-site. The journey doesn't have to start on the plate. Chips can be planted at the food's point of origin, tracking where it came from, its freshness, and when your smart fridge should restock. I just hope these chips don't have any sharp edges . . . ouch.
- Cisco's consumer version of its corporate Telepresence hardware enables high-definition conference calling from your living room. That can eliminate long lines and travel to and from health screenings. Doctors could do exams from any-

where. Someday, these machines could interface with in-home medical screening devices to monitor heart, breathing, blood pressure, and other vitals. Many of these functions could be done today with existing technologies like Skype and PC-linked gadgets.

To achieve the scale needed to make a dent in the U.S. health care system, though, insurers and employers will need to put the right incentives in place for individuals and doctors to adopt these technologies. Buried deep inside NutriSmart's ingestible chip is a business case. Don't stay up waiting for digital signals from Warren Buffett's colon. He can afford as many doctor visits as he wants. Unfortunately, there are plenty of others who would ingest an entire circuit board if they could save $30 a month on the obscene cost of health insurance.

Power to the (Chinese) People

Watching a corpulent couple streaming YouTube videos on a flight to Florida, I find it's hard to think of the U.S. as an underdog. When you think about the masses of low-wage factory workers in China or cheerful Indian phone reps working the 3:00 A.M. shift, you don't think, "We need to kick their ass!" No matter how stark the differences, our fates are intertwined. The key to U.S. recovery is in fueling their ascension, not fighting it. And, I don't mean by buying their gadgets on credit. We tried that already. I literally mean *fueling*. The single biggest growth opportunity for U.S. companies is to enable China to be energy independent, not the United States. Let me explain why.

Hey, Big Spender   The U.S. has a mature infrastructure that needs upgrades and repair, but it *has* an infrastructure. China is building much of its own from scratch as it struggles to keep up with success and stay ahead of chaos. Plus, it's sitting on piles of U.S. dollars that it wants to turn into sustainable assets. Already, China is the world's biggest green energy consumer. Not only will it have 10 million electric car charging stations by 2020, in 2010 it invested $54.4 billion in wind, solar, and other renewable energy technologies. That number has increased by 50 percent for two years. By comparison, the U.S. spent $34 billion, while Germany spent $41.2 billion.

The difference is that the United States makes its investments with borrowed money while Germany and China fund theirs with growth. One is a sustainable source of investment, the other, not so much.

Easy Sale   To a company that sells green tech, a customer is a customer no matter if they eat pancakes or rice porridge with pig's liver for breakfast. But, the business case is much easier to make for new construction than for upgrades. According to oil historian (my next job) Daniel Yergen, the United States is already 80 percent energy independent. Home and factory energy is generally affordable, domestically produced, and increasingly renewable. The remaining 20 percent is fuel for cars. Fuel standards and electric engines could get the U.S. to energy independence by 2040. Converting U.S. homes and offices to green energy with a 10-year breakeven point is a much tougher sale than creating green factories, subway systems, or apartment complexes in China.

Price-Sensitive Consumer   With 1.4 billion people, every watt counts. People in emerging markets are extremely price sensitive, so an LCD TV that saves $50 a year on electricity will beat the pants off an energy-guzzling plasma every time. In the U.S., that same 52-inch TV can be left on all weekend and most middle-class families wouldn't think to administer a spanking or a week of hard labor to the offending child.

Efficiency-oriented technology will be the ultimate test of America's innovation engine. Sure, Google can make a great web site, but if it (or any other company) finds a way to make thousands of servers run at one-fifth of the energy, a long line of global businesses will show up bearing gifts. It won't be easy; every country wants a piece of the bulging energy wallet.

A Little Something for Everyone   Fortunately, you don't have to be an energy company with huge R&D to play in this space. You won't even need an underwater drill or one of those sexy, rubber orange jumpsuits. New energy opportunities will span borders and industries with something for every kind of entrepreneur. In Table 5.1, I classify them in five categories that vary in how complex, big, and exportable resulting innovations might be.

Table 5.1   Energy Innovation Opportunities

Complexity	Higher	Application and recycling	Generation and distribution storage
	Lower	Information	Conservation
		Lower	Higher
		size and exportability	

1. **Information:** Data continues to revolutionize every industry. Enron aside, energy will be no different. Trading commodities and pollution credits will be part of it, but the biggest innovations will, in some way, be tied to physical infrastructure. Companies like EnerNOC Inc. are already using data to optimize energy use, get better deals from suppliers, and track and trade greenhouse emissions. Better measurement and reporting can apply throughout the entire energy supply chain. Improved geological data, weather forecasting, and modeling will help reinvent how efficiently energy gets generated—or even how much less annoying your weatherman can be.

2. **Conservation:** Data will only take you so far. The fundamentals of consumption don't change; you *will* drive somewhere, you *will* charge your laptop, and you *will* watch *Golden Girls* reruns. Companies that have an interest in employees or customers not wasting energy need to develop incentive programs and reward systems to achieve the right behaviors. I'll talk more about this in the IncentiveNation chapter. There is also an exportable part to conservation. New technologies can sit on top of existing infrastructure to reduce consumption. At the high end, Japan's Chugoku Electric Power Company exports and installs high-efficiency chillers, boilers, hybrid water heaters, and LED lighting technology to customers like the Amari Hotels in Thailand. At the lower end, companies like Energenie produce outlet adapters that keep appliances like TVs from consuming power while not being used . . . and presumably plotting to overthrow humanity.

3. **Application and recycling:** Everywhere you look, there are energy-saving technologies from reusable containers to bicycles to rechargeable batteries. Let's face it, most are not living up to their potential. There are plenty of unexplored creative ways to apply technology that already exists to conserve, create,

and store energy. One of my favorite examples is Pavegen Systems, which installed sensors in the floor of a London nightclub to generate 60 percent of the club's electricity. The company is expanding into universities and public spaces with high foot traffic. Not only is this a huge cost saving, but an entire ecosystem for selling, installing, and servicing these kinds of technologies will emerge, especially overseas, where it will have more industrial uses.

4. **Storage:** Lots of big companies are eyeing the energy storage business. As we use more wind, solar, and other intermittent technologies, there need to be better ways to store it. Unless someone figures out how to get the sun out at night, this will be a big business for the foreseeable future. As batteries die or get replaced and thrown out, there will be new and creative businesses to manage that lifecycle. Japanese companies and a few in the U.S., like Intel and GE, are going hard after this space.

5. **Generation and distribution:** Understandably, milking clean, renewable energy from nature gets the most attention from energy companies, investors, and government. The opportunity to replace coal and oil is massive and everyone wants in. Transmitting that energy to people efficiently is another mounting challenge. Massive, complex, smart-grid projects are part of the opportunity. The other might be wireless energy transmission. It is already being used to power or charge small devices. Soon, it could eliminate most cables and cords. Your cell phone is already cooking our gonads, what's a few more invisible kilowatts between friends?

The following are a couple of ideas I think are promising in generation and distribution.

The Sun Is Free   When I was 8 years old, my parents bought me a Sharp solar-powered calculator. It didn't take long for me to break and dismember it. I was fascinated by how thin the solar cell was. Even then, I wondered what would happen if everything was coated with this stuff. Finally, solar is becoming economically viable. There are lots of competing technologies, but the big winners will be ones that scale, can be retrofit on existing structures, and don't need to link to a power grid. In the same way emerging markets went straight to mobile phones instead of running phone wires, energy will skip right to wireless, standalone technologies in Asia, India, and Latin America. When it happens, tens of millions of people will join the modern economy as producers and consumers. Google is taking the lead by investing $280 million in SolarCity, a solar rooftop installation firm. That's on top of the $168 million it invested in a massive solar generation project in the Mojave Desert. Other companies better follow suit before oil goes through the roof or Google buys the sun.

After a decade of broken promises, solar paint will soon be viable. For now, thin-film is the best alternative. It can be used on roofs, windows, and someday on your Ford Focus. First Solar, an Arizona company, manufactures some of the better ones. It has many successful installations in Germany and other parts of the world. Another promising technology already in the market is Dow Chemical's solar roof shingles. They are so simply designed, a petulant child could install them. Only the final plug-in requires an electrician.

Invisible Power, Everywhere   We are bombarded by more than just sunlight. All movement could, in theory, be harnessed—wind, ocean waves, wireless signals, human motion, static electricity, moving water in plumbing, a chatty neighbor, you name it. Some of these things are already being turned into power. Intel is working on tiny, wearable sensors that can capture energy from body heat and sunlight. This gives a whole new meaning to the words "power tie." Simon Fraser University in Vancouver developed a way to capture energy from human movement, specifically walking. This technology could reduce the size and weight of batteries that soldiers or emergency workers carry. The Canadian military signed on as the first client. (Perhaps they will power the Celine Dion radio each soldier is required to carry.) Sweden's Jernhusen designed a system of vents and sensors to capture surplus body heat from commuters at a high-traffic train station to warm a nearby office building, reducing energy costs by 25 percent.

So What?

There is nothing new about looking abroad for opportunities. Companies have done that for years. What is new is how much of our growth and success will now be linked to foreign markets and their money. For too long, U.S. innovation turned inward; selling salad shooters to American insomniacs has run its course. Now, the tough job begins. Getting emerging markets to want what we make will be our toughest innovation challenge yet—and the only path to growth.

In a philosophical sense, no one needs growth. Whether you're a huge company or a small entrepreneur, if you make enough to be comfortable, you could stop there. Why not open just one Subway sandwich location? Can't Apple be satisfied with only selling computers? Why expand into phones or digital content? It's human nature to want more, make more, and suck the earth dry doing it. Scarcity and the rising costs that go with it are the checks and balances on infinite consumption. They are also the fuel for innovation. They force us to work within limits and find creative ways to substitute, conserve, and reuse. No one's had to be more resourceful (a better term for innovative) than poor people in emerging markets. For a little inspiration, watch the Reuters video of slum-dwelling Filipinos making indoor lights out of water, bleach, and empty soda bottles. It's an idea originally devised by MIT. As some emerge from those slums, will the first light bulb they buy be made by a U.S. company?

If our future lies in making things, wouldn't it make sense to have a nation of makers, not consumers? The next chapter is all about how to create such a place.

CHAPTER 6

Make Makers

Let's face it: Education is about preparing little Johnny to earn a living. Yes, there are a few lifers who get to stay in school forever. That's great if you're Jill Gates or get adopted by Warren Buffett (as I've been trying to do for nearly a decade). A rich country can afford to lean back and drag its greasy fingers across the screen of an iPad. An indebted one needs makers. I define a maker as someone who creates something the marketplace needs. For the foreseeable future, it's builders, engineers, designers, and technologists. It could also be an entrepreneur who creates a successful business or an artisan who makes furniture, jewelry, or custom kites. The best kinds of makers, for our purposes, are ones who make things that can be exported, scaled, and employ people.

As bad as it seems to be shackled to an assembly line in Guangdong, those workers have a connectedness to the physical world we've long forgotten. Just like money makes money, a maker economy will continually spawn jobs and create exportable innovations in tech, energy, and manufacturing. To make makers, education needs to be rehabilitated. Instead of treating a broken education system as some big, festering disease, I'd like to reframe it as a 10-year business challenge. That means making the remedies actionable and profitable for businesses. Not only will better graduates make better employees, but they'll eventually become higher spending customers. With strained local budgets and a withering middle class, companies must take on the education challenge to secure their own domestic future.

So what should businesses, entrepreneurs, and individuals do to rebuild America's maker culture? My strategy comes in five simple steps with a free toy in every box:

1. Fix the core (redefine the curriculum and decide who learns what)
2. Automate learning
3. Repair school financing
4. Make makers (spawn the next generation of producers)
5. Create micropreneurs (we'll cover this in the next chapter)

Before jumping into specific opportunities, let's start with the problems.

Education Complications

Like a May-December romance in a Woody Allen movie, education and market demand have drifted apart. Now, economic conditions threaten to turn the drifting into drowning.

Rich Kid/Poor Kid

In the precollege years, kids with demanding parents, posh school districts, and ambition do well. Others are trapped inside outdated learning models. As they move on to college, they pay dearly for a bloated system that's out of line with demand. It's a system that still churns out boatloads of journalism, literature, and film majors when good jobs in those professions play out more like a perverse lottery than a career. At the same time, shortages of nurses, engineers, and designers abound. Maybe that's because nurses rarely appear on Bravo (maybe on Cinemax, but I'm almost certain those aren't real nurses).

Despite all this, the well off will adapt and have the clout to demand better results. Though financially insulated, they aren't immune to the economic challenges coming in the next decade. The bigger challenges lie on the side of the street that's lined with graffiti.

Like an insufficient funds fee when your balance is already zero, the recession added insult to injury to those stuck in the public education system. Growing competition in tech, science, and mathematics, finds many middle class and poor kids falling short. Changes in demand for labor are forcing us to rethink education just when the government is running out of IOUs.

When I'm not writing books, developing new businesses, or rescuing kittens from burning buildings, I volunteer for Junior Achievement. It's a terrific nonprofit that brings business professionals into classrooms to teach success skills. I've taught grades 9 to 12 once a week for 14 years in New York City public schools. I'd sum up my experience this way: I'm concerned about our future. Seventy percent of the time, I'm greeted by an indifferent or exhausted veteran teacher. The other 30 percent are youthful and optimistic. They're either marching toward exasperation or killing time until a high-paying suburban job opens up. All are equally thrilled to let me give them a weekly, one-hour vacation. Of the 35 kids in each class, there are usually five standouts, mostly girls. They participate, ask questions, and absorb new concepts. Then, there's the lumpy middle. They show little interest. Sometimes, there is a quiet diamond in the rough. Finally, every class has two or three kids who stepped right out of *The Shawshank Redemption*. They're usually taller than me, have full beards, or kids of their own (presumably in a neighboring Junior Achievement class). If I'm lucky, they'll skip class or sleep in the back. If I'm unlucky, I'll spend all my time disciplining them or explaining to police the events leading up to the fire.

Aggregate results seem to validate my observations. Almost half the students in the 50 largest school districts never get a high school diploma. As for the ones in school, the Institute for Education Sciences tested 15-year-olds across 41 countries in math, reading, and science. Americans consistently ranked somewhere between celery and Slovenia.* China, Finland, Canada, Japan, and even Latvia consistently beat the U.S., which came in 16th to 31st among tested countries. The good news? Only six of our kids tried to eat their ScanTron forms. Go USA!

The facilities in public schools aren't any better. I usually walk out of my Junior Achievement classes covered with chalk dust. My colleagues think I narrowly escaped an aborted Colombian drug deal. Public school facilities were great for teaching in 1984, not in 2012. Public colleges vary, but most are nowhere near what I

---

*http://nces.ed.gov/surveys/international/ide/.

experience walking into, say, MIT. There, I'm greeted by a LEGO robot that's more functional as most members of my family. Not so at public institutions. Most financing relies on local taxes. If you happen to live in a poor area, everyone will be covered in chalk for decades. You can only get so creative when tied to the current model, public budgets, and facilities. Unless we pay off our debt or eliminate military spending, the answer lies in new learning models that are automated, and in some cases, privately run. I explore a few of these in the next section.

Collidge Challinjiz

The problems don't end in high school. Lurking behind good state, city, and private colleges are too many expensive cafeterias selling burgers and lies. These schools take thousands of dollars from students who could barely get out of high school. And, the results are creating a generation of unemployees.

Graduation Rates Are Dropping   According to the *New York Times*, only 33 to 44 percent of the kids who start at a top university in the U.S. graduate within six years. Overall, only half of those who enroll end up with a degree. Those in the bottom 40 percent in high school are unlikely to graduate at all. Among developed countries, only Italy does worse, but at least there your mom will cook you pasta and do your laundry well into your 40s.

Not Ready   In New York state, for example, only 23 percent of 1.3 million high school graduates in 2007 were ready for college-level work, according to state education officials. On the bright side, almost all were ready for beer pong.

Falling Enrollment   The U.S. dropped from second place to 13th out of 34 countries in the number of students enrolled in university. We placed 25th in math and 17th in science enrollments. China was first.

Graduating Dumb ... and Poor   According to a 2006 Pew study, 50 percent of college seniors scored below proficient in basic analytical skills.*

---

*http://chronicle.com/free/v54/i34/34b01701.htm.

The cost of education has skyrocketed. The average private college tuition is over $26,000 a year. It's $18,500 for nonresidents attending state schools and $7,000 for residents. The average student leaves school $20,000 in debt.

A Disconnect   While incomes have barely risen in the last 30 years, the cost of both public and private tuition has increased 225 percent. If the education were so much better, wouldn't the opportunity reflect that? As Figure 6.1 shows, the two biggest fields expected to grow are education and health care, but their salaries don't exactly scream, "Get a college education!" Aside from tech and professional services, most of the higher paying industries are tiny and slow growing.

We Don't Need No Education   At the current trajectory, health care, education, and professional/tech services are expected to create the most jobs in the next decade. Most of the jobs expected to be created will pay below $50,000 a year. That makes you wonder, is college even necessary? If not, is there a better way to spend four years and thousands of dollars? Figure 6.2 shows the stark, yawning gap between tuition and wages for college graduates from 1980 to 2008.

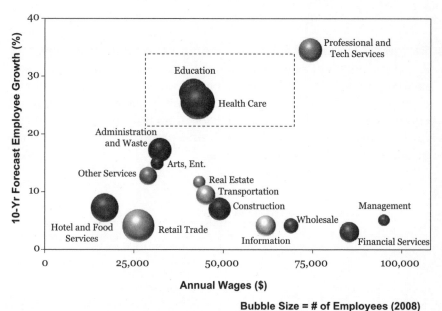

Figure 6.1   Expected U.S. Sector Growth Rates
Source: Bureau of Labor Statistics (BLS).

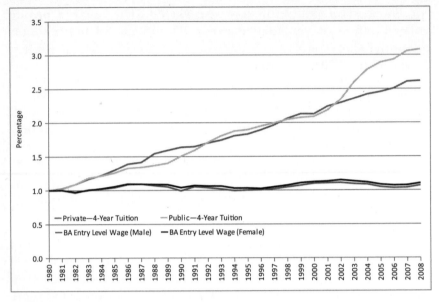

Figure 6.2   Real Growth of College Tuition and Wages for College Graduates
Source: U.S. College Board.

Shortages and Surpluses   Diplomas can be purchased in many flavors—literature, finance, or cookie dough. The reasons might vary, but salaries, costs, and admissions rarely align with actual demand. For example, many medical device and energy sector manufacturers complain that they're ready to hire *and train* hundreds of employees for high paying jobs, but they can't find people with the right skills or aptitude. See Table 6.1.

Table 6.1   Careers in Flux

Too Many . . .	Too Few . . .
Lawyers	Nurses
Entertainers	Engineers
Bankers	Skilled tradesmen
Journalists	Doctors
Social media experts	Designers
Marketers	Computer programmers
MBAs	Security experts

Table 6.2   How a Disobedient Economy Will Affect Education

Economic Trajectory	Player	How They're Impacted by Economic Trends
Positive	Private Schools	• Perception advantage in competitive labor market • Capital and technology advantage
	Employers	• Cheap labor bonanza • Have resources to acquire needed skills
	Education Tech Developers	• Can bring needed scale and automation • Can enable capital to replace expensive labor
	Trade Schools	• Offer flexibility and labor force re-tooling
Mixed	Parents	• Middle class pinched on education cost • Tougher choices
	Online Educators	• Can compete on price if reputations are cleaned up
	Good Students	• Less debt • More choices • Fewer high paying careers
	Teachers	• Need new skills • Top teachers in rich communities will earn top dollar, public school teachers will not
Negative	Poor and Minorities	• Less access to high-quality education
	Public Schools	• Budget cuts • Stricter standards

Winners and Losers in the Next 10 Years

As public budgets are cut and people re-evaluate the sticker shock of a top-flight education, plenty of opportunities will open up. As you can see in Table 6.2, the current trajectory creates a patchwork of winners, losers, and a few parties caught in between.

The rest of this chapter is all about new ways to exploit the power of businesses and individuals to re-imagine education. It's not as daunting as you'd think. Some groundbreaking models and technologies are already there and begging to be scaled. And some old ideas are worth another look, like a forgotten Beatles B side.

Fix the Core

A system that now cranks out failure needs to start churning out self-actualized makers. That journey starts with questioning some stale assumptions all of us grew up with.

Come for Four, Stay for Two

Stephen Trachtenberg and Gerald Kauvar, professors at George Washington University, wrote in the *New York Times* about getting a college degree in three years. In fact, Northwestern Law School offers a two-year degree and Texas Tech can get you a medical degree in three. I doubt three-year grads are any more likely to remove the wrong kidney or stitch a Junior Mint inside a patient than their four-year counterparts.

Like candy with vitamins, this is a win for everyone. Schools get to use wasted, empty buildings during summers, students pay less tuition, and education is delivered more concisely. Imagine the cost of college instantly dropping by 25 percent. The authors argue that schools would make even more money because three-year students clear out faster, allowing new, fresh tuitions to come in. The professors ask: Why can't this be applied to all colleges, not just grad schools? It can. It wouldn't have to be mandatory. Those that do can bring a wave of innovation to their schools that would resemble the real world, not a four-year cocoon.

Why not do the same for elementary and high school? Who says high school must take four years? Some are inching towards this. Texas recently passed the "Doogie Howser Amendment," which allows kids to graduate high school early if they score well on advanced placement tests (or get cast in a cheesy TV sitcom). Students who qualify instantly save the school system money and get to move on with their lives, rather than spend another year pining away for the cheerleader. (Remember, kids, college has cheerleaders, too.) Texas legislators couldn't do this alone. Texas A&M University and the University of Texas agreed to manage the admission criteria and accept students who make the cut. The next step for Texas might be to get those same colleges to let their students graduate earlier and for less.

Bard High School Early College in Manhattan takes a different path. It's a combo school. It gives kids a high school and two-year college degree in four years. Bard successfully shaved two years off high school by offering a rigorous, aggressive curriculum. Bard College, which partnered with the New York Board of Education to create the school, opened a second location in Queens and plans to open up to 150 more as it applies for federal funding.

These schools show there's plenty of room for others to innovate. If schools like Bard connected with universities in each state, we could shave two years off education subsidies for state colleges. Private colleges can make similar arrangements with public or private schools. In fact, employers can partner with schools the same way. If they can influence the curriculum and qualifications, they could take early graduates from colleges or even high school. The college gets a successful placement and can accept the next student in line. The U.S. gets a new taxpayer sooner. If 30 percent of each year's 3 million high school grads started earning $24,000, by year three, this new workforce would produce more than $20 billion in annual tax revenue (assuming a 15 percent tax rate).*

"The Commonsense Centrifuge"

Over the last few decades an intellectual dishonesty has crept into almost everything. Education, especially, is wrapped in debilitating political correctness. For example, I was teaching a 9th grade Junior Achievement class and could not get one boy to stop cracking jokes and distracting everyone. I spent the first 10 minutes of a 50-minute class trying to quiet him down. Finally, I told him to stand outside the classroom. After five minutes of forward movement, the teacher brought my pint-sized nemesis back in. She informed me that I'm not allowed to kick anyone out of class because it's considered "corporal punishment." I wondered if there was another term for robbing 34 other kids of an education. Unfortunately, you can't call 911 for education theft.

Similarly, it doesn't take long to identify top performers or those with niche talents like memorization, piano, or smooth talking. The system rarely knows when to send one kid to pharmacy school, another to study music, and the third to become Jay-Z. New York City does test kids as young as five for gifted classes. However, it's on the hunt for a new way to test. School officials believe the current tests are being hacked by parents, who extensively prepare their kids and no doubt, promise them more love and Transformers than their nongifted siblings. New York's system also overlays test results with confusing racial quotas, district admission minimums, and other

---

*Author analysis using data from Bureau of Labor Statistics, www.bls.gov.

peripheral criteria. Like those random searches at the airport, we're achieving something less than excellence. To bring the best kids to market faster, empowered, well-trained teachers could do just as well. There needs to be a "commonsense centrifuge," a flexible way of identifying students with different needs and placing them into classes that develop those skills for real careers. Many companies already use the Myers-Briggs test to match personality types with the right jobs, bosses, and coworkers. The same opportunity exists for schools. Once we know which kids are scholastically inclined and which are not, we can automate and customize their curriculum.

Redefine What's Essential

The College Board, which administers Advanced Placement (AP) exams, is moving from having kids memorize every known element to focusing on broader concepts and critical thinking. With content freely available online and automation for grammar and fact-based learning around the corner, schools can focus on teaching what really matters. Those things are critical thinking, problem solving, math, science, finance, ethics, and creativity.

Teach Creativity and Critical Thinking   IBM polled 1,500 CEOs who ranked creativity as the top leadership competency for solving business problems. Unfortunately, the U.S. system is moving backward. While the U.S. focuses on standardized test scores, other countries are revamping their curriculum around creativity, the fuel for innovation. In fact, England is revamping all its subjects to focus on generating ideas to solve real-world problems. China is starting to do the same. The European Union is implementing creativity programs using the Torrance Tests of Creative Thinking to measure progress. A high childhood Torrance score has a three times stronger correlation to creative success as an adult than does a high IQ. In the United States, some innovative private models are also popping up. The Blue School was started by members of the Blue Man Group (yes, grown men painted blue). The school focuses on developing creativity and lets kids choose parts of the curriculum. It's important to make the distinction between the skill of creativity and a career in a creative field. Creativity can and should be applied across multiple disciplines.

Teach Finance   Every time I take up a new Junior Achievement class, it amazes me how little kids are taught about money—saving, budgeting, investing, credit, and so on. I attended a New York public high school, majored in business at New York University, and I still had to learn investing and budgeting on the gritty streets. Okay, it was actually from old *Consumer Reports* investing issues, but you get the idea. According to a Pew study, only 20 percent of college seniors had just the basic quantitative skills. Most could not evaluate a credit card offer. This is an opportunity for financial companies to step in and offer classes and start building goodwill with their future customers, as long as they don't sell the kids any Collateralized Diploma Obligations.

Align with Demand

The number of jobs available is not aligned with school admissions for those professions. Schools churn out lawyers, actors, and journalists just because they can pay, even if it means their parents will live off canned tuna and the kindness of strangers in retirement. If schools don't do this on their own, there is an opportunity to create a demand-pay index that tracks and projects demand and salaries in each profession. It should also track successful placements and graduate earnings over time. A tuition-salary ratio for each school and major would be a good start. Eventually, this will force education prices and durations down for professions that pay $20,000 when school costs $80,000.

Rate Schools Like Investments

At these prices, school is the biggest investment of time and money anyone will ever make. Isn't it time we started to treat them exactly like investments? Just as Morningstar rates mutual funds, there is a need for a similar online rating system for schools that goes well beyond what *BusinessWeek* does for business schools. From schools with circular saws to those with girls named Muffy, there's a need to weed out shady or overpriced institutions. This system could:

- Measure school effectiveness in placement, as well as employer reviews of candidates from different schools.
- Show actual placement ratios and salaries.

- Offer a recruiting hub for employers that works just like scouting in pro sports; let them check student grades and statistics and see which ones they want to interview. Make it social so kids can put up introductory videos and sample projects.
- Provide comparison shopping for students on everything from vocational classes to the male to female ratio.

Make Programs Resizeable

Whether its law, writing, or construction, education should be linked to demand based on national and local employer surveys. If construction hiring slows, so should the number of seats available. This retooling of schools can be sponsored by employers who might get a first-look deal at top graduates, as well as other benefits. Businesses and schools can work together to project likely hiring and salaries, so schools can plan their curricula accordingly. That should lead to better pricing for the education. Though it's safe to say no drama major should ever pay full price.

This kind of collaboration is not impossible. The Cincinnati Strive Together program created a successful "cradle to career" ecosystem. Educators from preschool through college got together with government officials and employers to share data, set common goals, and develop a plan to solve for low college enrollment. Eventually, their ambitions expanded to overall preparedness. Sounds fluffy, but the results have been good. In three years, kindergarten readiness, fourth grade reading and math, and high school graduation rates are all up between 7 and 14 percent.

Automate: Rise of the Machines

Federal stimulus money propped up a lot of state budgets (and I'm sure bought at least a few cronies new Audis). It was a huge missed opportunity. Education was 12 percent of the stimulus. Every state received more than $250 per capita for education—enough to get a computer or iPad for every child and teacher. Instead, some districts, like one in North Carolina, used it to pay for theme parks and movies. With the stimulus gone, school budgets look like Swiss cheese. States will seek out privately funded schools to save money. Fortunately, those schools are much easier to do business with. What is that business? Automation.

Consider video stores: leaving your home, getting in your car, and driving to a mall to retrieve one shiny disc. That concept will seem implausible to the next generation of kids. (And good luck explaining rewinding.) That is exactly how standing in front of a class teaching kids facts or math will be perceived in 20 years. The time and physical distance between a question and the answer is disappearing. Remember that actor from that movie with the kid who had a Dalmatian in Cincinnati? All you have to do is type that nonsense into your phone and no more agonizing; problem solved. In less than 50 years, that data will feed directly into your brain, in a bloodless, phoneless experience. Until then, facts will continue getting closer and closer to your brain. Storing them inside your brain will seem as odd as wheeling all your possessions around in a shopping cart everywhere you go.

The days of education scarcity are over. The Internet has created so much content and so many ways to distribute it that the idea of a classroom now seems somewhat quaint and pointless. Any fact-based subject—math, science, English, or even sex ed—can be taught better using technology that adjusts to each student's pace in ways teaching a class of 35 kids never could. In the next decade, there will be no better way to have fewer, more highly paid teachers focused on critical thinking. Following are some of the ways benevolent Terminators can replace people teaching facts.

Software as Teacher

One of the hottest players in automated learning is Knewton, a software tool tested at the University of Arizona in 2011. It adapts to each student by rewarding right answers with new knowledge or repeating material after wrong answers. (A feature to Tase anyone who tries to goof off on Facebook is optional.) The interface looks like a video game, but tracks skill development and provides customized help. It costs $150 per student per course and can be offered remotely or in-class. This could be a huge opportunity. Entire school districts would pay a fraction of the cost of live teaching. Tools like this could even reward kids with SMS messages, gaming currency, or points redeemable for free lunches or educational toys. Niche players like Rosetta Stone are also well positioned to enter the automated education business using its foreign language software.

Take This Tablet

For now, the iPad is the only game in town. Android, Motorola, or others might eventually catch up—if they can develop targeted uses for a tablet besides porn. Education is a noble one to try. The iPad alone has over 20,000 educational apps, and iTunes U has over 250,000 lectures, podcasts, and full courses on every possible subject. Some schools, like the University of Oklahoma, have conducted unstructured experiments giving iPads to students. Educational benefits were, at best, anecdotal. Still, all this information and capability is begging to be organized and packaged as a scaled, automated, learning curriculum. Developers can easily do this in partnership with schools. Amazon with its low-priced Kindle is best positioned to take a leading position in education, especially as the reader evolves into a full-fledged tablet.

Reinvent and Repackage Content

Remember when people sold Britannica encyclopedias door to door for $2,500 a set? Now, Wikipedia has scores more articles that, on balance, are far more accurate and up to date. Flaws and criticisms aside, Wikipedia alone could be the basis of all K–12 educational content. It would be a huge upgrade from the moldy textbooks that are passed around for years in public schools. Others are offering more niche options, like the *Economist*'s business courses on emerging markets or Google and Mozilla's courses on how to code. MIT made much of its course content available for free on iTunes.

The challenge is packaging this free, high-quality information to replace textbooks, which are expensive, out of date, and depressingly inert. Major textbook publishers have partnered to offer CourseSmart, an app that lets students download textbooks, highlight, and write notes in them. CafeScribe does something similar, but also connects you to a social network where you can share notes with other students reading the same book. Inkling has similar features to CafeScribe, but lets students buy books by the chapter and has interactive quizzes and live notes updates. FlexBooks is an open source project that is most promising because it uses packaged content from the Web to deliver custom, affordable textbooks that are always up to date and free of mysterious stains and scribbles. Of course, the gorilla in the room is Amazon, which in mid-2011 began textbook rentals on its Kindle platform.

Hardware Distribution Models

Computer hardware has gotten so cheap that it hardly makes sense not to buy it, but Google is attempting a new model that packages applications and support with Chrome-based netbooks. At $20 per month for education, it's an interesting approach that has potential. Of course, education is not Google's core business. Schools are high-touch customers, so there will be plenty of room for competition for different variations on this. There is no reason Dell or HP couldn't enter the space using their tablet or PC assets plus Knewton software. They each have sales forces that can make this happen.

The One Laptop Per Child (OLPC) program, originally intended as a $100 purchase, actually costs about $260 per child to deploy and $20 per year to maintain. Several million PCs have been distributed worldwide. The project also spawned several competing initiatives. An Indian company claimed to be able to produce a $35 laptop, but realized that would only cover the cost of a laptop bag. It finally demonstrated a working tablet using the Android operating system but is struggling to get it to market. The United States is crying out for a developed market version that uses game dynamics coupled with testing modules and other advanced tools to get students plugged into the digital economy. While far from perfect, just getting PCs into students' hands opens incredible possibilities. In Uruguay, laptops from OLPC allow kids to teach their parents to read. Farmers borrow their kids' laptops to check prices for grains to ensure they get a fair price in the market. On the downside, OLPC inadvertently gave kids access to porn. Welcome to unfettered freedom, Uruguay.

Mobile and Remote Learning

Does education need a building? Or, could you stagger classes better if transportation to a school wasn't always necessary? Suddenly, mass-home-schooling can be as good as showing up and having a grey burger for lunch. Top universities already offer online learning, though you probably won't get to hit on the cute girl in your online marketing class. Abilene Christian University (ACU) gave students iPods, iPhones, and iPads to "flip the classroom." Students watch or listen to lectures on the go and work through problems in class. Khan Academy used a similar concept to deliver online learning in almost every elementary and high school subject. Salman Khan developed thousands of online educational videos and interactive exercises. Students watch lectures at home and do interactive homework. This model plants the seeds of a self-directed education system that can scale. You don't always need fancy gadgets or speedy bandwidth. Carnegie Mellon's MILLEE Project uses simple mobile games to teach language in India and China. Others just use text messaging.

It's Just a Game

It's no secret that kids love video games. They're in luck. The future of education will have avatars, high scorers, and social sharing . . . with trash talk. You won't have to kill pigs with angry birds, but you might have to count how long your ammunition will last or calculate launch angles. Gaming is ideal for teaching facts and testing experientially. If the games are competitive, public scores will drive accountability and better performance through competition. This is the next frontier for scalable, digestible education. And most of this gaming can happen at home. The classroom will be reserved for discussion and critical thinking—a reversal of logic that can't come soon enough. One interesting example of game-based education is an online game called MoneyIsland. It was designed by an accomplished teacher from Washington, D.C. The game performs the small miracle of making it fun for kids to learn finance and planning. Instead of being marketed to consumers, it's being sold to schools, nonprofits, and financial institutions that can use it to fulfill their criteria for the Community Reinvestment Act.

Think any of this automation talk is farfetched for the U.S.? It will happen in the next few years. Why? South Korea is already there. The country is taking its entire school system digital and paperless by 2015. It's replacing all textbooks with tablets and putting an emphasis on remote learning via these devices. American innovators, your turn.

Repair School Financing

I could write chapters on what's wrong with school affordability, but I'm trying to stick to things businesses and people can do something about. Briefly, I'll mention the importance of fixing college financing. The biggest reason tuitions shot through the roof is that banks are willing to lend virtually unlimited amounts to students at ultralow rates. Why? They have no risk. Banks successfully lobbied to keep students from defaulting on tuition loans. Today, if a student stops paying, the government pays. Banks continue handing out cash as schools soak up every last penny by raising tuitions. As more students default, they carry bad credit scores around forever, like scarlet letters. Change seems unlikely as powerful interests will defend their huge stake in the current system.

We need a tuition recession. Phasing out all loan guarantees except to poor students and allowing others to default is the only way to stop tuition increases cold. Lenders will have to manage risk again. They can use SAT scores, majors, graduation rates, and other metrics to decide which schools and students are loan-worthy. Most schools will get cheaper and more creative as the inefficient ones close. This approach will also help align tuitions with market demand. For example, art history majors will qualify for smaller loans than those who plan to study engineering.

Save Better

There's room for innovation in tuition cost control. Two of the most interesting ideas that rose from the cauldron of school financing were prepaid tuition plans and the CollegeSure CD. Prepaid plans are typically offered by state schools to allow parents to lock in or at least manage the future cost of college by prepaying tuition. The prepayment comes at a rate higher than current tuition, but you come out ahead by the fourth or fifth year. The problem with these plans is you're committing to a particular state's schools, and you have to commit big money early. The CollegeSure CD was created by the state of Montana. It lets you save for any school at a rate linked to tuition cost increases. Historically, that's been double the rate of inflation. The downside is private tuitions go up faster. So if your child chooses Princeton instead of Montana State, you might wish you never bought that LEGO set.

Public Relations

Companies are well aware of the power of good PR. Mark Zuckerberg set up a $100 million fund for Newark public schools. He did it around the time of the release of *The Social Network,* which portrayed him in an unflattering light. Other companies do this as a normal part of business. Intel, for example, plans to donate $100 million for university research. There can be a hollowness to donations that feed an existing system with questionable results. The bigger opportunity is to donate funds in ways that drive change. Creating jobs for local graduates, creating custom curricula for high-demand careers, or earmarking funds for learning technologies discussed previously can add a substantive wrinkle to what has historically been a valuable, but one-dimensional, PR activity.

Empower Makers

Without a college degree, eventually the high school hero bows to the geek he used to store in his locker. We live in a time when "revenge of the jocks" would be a perfectly reasonable movie premise. Against impossible odds, even the most scholastically challenged jocks try to get college degrees. And plenty of schools will take their money. As of 2011, 31 percent of loans to community college students were in default, compared to 25 percent for all student loans. For decades, even the least scholarly were sold on the mythical value of a degree. It was a powerful, multiyear campaign not unlike what DeBeers did with diamonds—make worthless crystals into something your fiancé would kill for. According to the Bureau of Labor Statistics (BLS), many people with a degree have a job that doesn't need one. See Table 6.3.

The BLS also projected job growth through 2018. With possible exceptions in professional services and finance, most of the jobs being created do not require a degree, especially not a four-year one.

As comedian Louis C.K. said, "Technical High School—that's where dreams get narrowed down. We tell our children, 'you can do anything you want' their whole lives. But at this place . . . we tell them, 'you can do eight things.' We got it down to eight for you."

Everyone's options get narrowed down eventually. A young Elton John wisely chose to perform "Tiny Dancer" rather than become a tiny dancer. Others need more help finding their purpose, training for it, and avoiding a four-year parking lot. Revamping vocational training, reviving apprenticeships, and aligning jobs with demand is

Table 6.3   Degrees in No-Degree-Needed Professions

Profession	Proportion with a College Degree
Flight attendants	29.8%
Retail salespersons	24.5%
Food service managers	24.1%
Customer service representatives	21.6%
Baggage porters and bellhops	17.4%
Secretaries (not legal/medical/executive)	16.6%
Hotel, motel, and resort desk clerks	16.1%
Telemarketers	15.8%
Taxi drivers and chauffeurs	15.2%
Mail carriers	13.9%
Telecommunications installers and repairers	13.1%
Manicurists and pedicurists	11.5%
Shampooers	11.5%
Locksmiths and safe repairers	10.2%

Source: Bureau of Labor Statistics (BLS).

just one part of the equation. The first and most important is making makers.

This paragraph is for the women reading (men, feel free to skip it). Have you ever gotten a flat tire while driving with your husband or boyfriend? Have you ever watched him stare and poke at the offending tire, as if his touch carried some magical healing properties? When he finally gives up and asks you to call AAA, do you remember feeling incredibly turned on? What if he grabbed a jack and a wrench and changed the tire in 10 minutes? (If you jumped out of the car and did it, you might as well book a Brazilian wax for two!) I bet he'd get a little extra lovin' that night for getting you to your daughter's high school graduation on time. I don't claim to speak for women, but I wonder how attractive it is watching a man tweet or gracefully sweep his fingers over an iPhone screen. I'm no macho Neanderthal, but there is a meek helplessness being bred into American society. On a macro level, that means relying on China to make all your things. On a micro level, it's relying on Jack, the Tire Guy, to get you to your kid's graduation. In both cases, they're things we should be able to do on our own. I think if you solve the micro problem, the macro one solves itself.

As unproductive industries shrink down to size, it's important we take the fear and mystery out of the industries that make things. That includes developing engineers who customize their own particle colliders and scientists who mix unstable compounds, explosions be damned. Builders can soon catch up to geeks and gamers, who already get to strut around like they knocked out Muhammad Ali (or maybe his sister).

Start Young . . . with Kindergarten Shop Class

I wasn't joking about the tires. And yes, I said kindergarten. Do I envision a circular saw in every classroom? Absolutely. Especially, if it means scraping that crusty lethargy off the U.S. economy. I am not alone. Deb Winsor, a Brooklyn carpenter, started a week-long program called Construction Kids where she teaches six-year-olds to build everything from log cabins to models of the White House. Over a dozen similar programs have sprung up around the country. Each features tiny fingers operating big hammers, drills, and buzz saws. And they love every minute of it. The Randall Museum in San Francisco teaches woodworking. The Eliot School in Boston teaches students to design and build furniture. The Tinkering School is a sleepaway camp for 8- to 17-year-olds in California who build sailboats and tree houses. Who would you rather be stuck on an island (or a project) with—a graduate of Yale Law or the Tinkering School?

Want to teach your children fractions? Have them measure and cut two-by-fours for their new tree house. If they get it wrong, the pieces won't fit. If you want to raise a successful architect or engineer, let your child sketch out plans for a soapbox car or a BattleBot. Learning by building in the real world is the kind of sensory experience computers can't replace. Having a physical object to show for your efforts is like getting an A in math that you can sit in or drive— and far more satisfying. That will translate into a generation of entrepreneurs, workers, and thinkers who are not afraid of a little dirt under their nails.

Lenore Skenazy, who champions this type of education, points out that kids are too used to perfect interfaces like the iPad. They need to learn how that perfection is achieved. The real world isn't perfect, so go ahead and saw, drill, or carve away the imperfect parts. Nolan Bushnell, co-founder of Atari, envisions clubs around the country that teach kids to make things and eventually get integrated into school programs. This is not unlike the LEGO Mindstorm robotics workshops that have sprung up around the country.

Even with the construction bubble long deflated, the maker wave can generate real revenues. One company, Inventables, in Chicago, sells supplies and materials to artists, inventors, and tinkerers. Home Depot and Best Buy are well positioned to become not only suppliers but also facilitators for makers. They can use their retail footprint to offer classes for hobbyists and connect makers with a manufacturing start-up engine. Some of those inventions can eventually be sold in their stores. Brands like Craftsman and Stanley can build child-safe tools designed for kindergarten builders. This field can eventually create even more opportunities for teachers, property owners, and insurers.

Makers, Amplified

In the 1970s and 80s, every sitcom featured at least one episode where a kid had to build a model volcano or solar system for a school science fair. Needless to say, clicking and snacking soundly killed off this relic. Very quietly, *Make* magazine is helping replace the science fair with the Maker Fair. It's a celebration of hackers, tinkerers, and do-it-yourselfers. Individuals and companies like Google and GE show off inventions from androids to medical monitors to hacked Guitar Hero instruments that can play real music.

Similar maker fairs are popping up elsewhere. A related movement of amateur biologists is documented in Marcus Wohlsen's book, *Biopunk: DIY Scientists Hack the Software of Life*. It's a grassroot, libertarian movement with attitude. The goal is to take science back from institutions. Many of the projects are self- or crowdfunded with participants sharing facilities and collaborating on research.

Collectively, we are witnessing the beginning of a new open source movement. The same rebellious explosion that created Linux, Firefox, and Wikipedia is breaking out in the science community. Instead of companies like Monsanto owning patents on seeds used to make food, the next generation of bio and tech inventions might just be open sourced. There is still room for companies to play alongside but in a different way. One way is to sponsor Maker facilities and competitions, build services and add-ons for biopunk inventions, facilitate project collaboration, and provide commercialization expertise for the gems that emerge. The Discovery Channel and shows like *Mythbusters* and *BattleBots* will continue to fuel this trend.

Redefine Vocational

Professor Robert Lerman of American University recommends teaching students how to behave and communicate professionally. A 2008 survey of over 2,000 businesses in Washington State found new employees could not solve problems, make decisions, resolve conflict, and negotiate, cooperate with others, and listen actively. Ouch. Retooling vocational training to teach these skills would be a good start. And why wait until community college? We used to call Brooklyn's Kingsborough Community College the 13th grade. Why not officially make it the 11th grade and build vocational training right into the high school curriculum? Schools should also facilitate networking online and on-site between students and professionals from various vocations. That way, students can get a feel for the jobs and the kinds of people doing them.

Teach Pride   Singapore's Institute of Technical Education (ITE) is an amazing turnaround story. For a long time, ITE was a punch line to a very sad joke. You'd rather tell your friends your son was in a romantic relationship with a llama than admit he went to trade school. If parental shame had an acronym, it would have been ITE (if it had a mascot, it might be a llama). The Singaporean government meticulously studied best practices of trade schools around the world and eventually turned these hair-design and beauty-therapy training centers into a national jewel. Now, graduates are sought after by top hotels, casinos, and hair salons. With their exemplary training, they out-compete cheaper foreign laborers. What made the difference? Teaching pride to those who are used to experiencing failure and condescension. Even if an ITE student sweeps a floor, that student is taught to be the best at it. With that attitude came respect and success.

There is no reason we couldn't have Singaporean-style ITEs here. Once those models are built they can franchise more easily than high-end colleges like Harvard or NYU, because their value isn't tied to scarcity or exclusivity.

Extend Vocational Options   Experts argue (that's what experts do) that undergrad business degrees are no more than expensive vocational training, especially majors like finance and marketing. It shouldn't cost between $80,000 and $200,000 to learn to work in groups and create PowerPoint presentations. Many of the lower ranked business schools barely require more than 10 hours of work a week. Even master's programs—liberal arts, social sciences, sub-top 50 MBAs, and some science degrees—are crimes against money. They don't produce extra earning potential and still rely on employers to teach core job skills. Mature graduates could have gone straight to the dance.

Mid-Career Tune-Ups

Not all education happens when you're young and trying to hook up with that cute girl or guy from shop class. Some of the most important education happens when you're an adult. Mature students have a powerful focus and commitment inspired by mortgage payments and the cost of raising kids.

iWoz a Programmer   Right here in the good old U.S.A., we've had a long history of successfully training people for completely new careers. In the early 1980s, computer programmers were hot (not George Clooney hot, Steve Wozniak hot). Back then, computers were the size of Buicks and had less computing power than my clock radio. Most of those jobs fizzled out as programming became more automated, but for a period of four to five years, the bubble created some real incomes. The same can be said for web design in the late 1990s and social media today.

Peer-Taught Upgrades   When I was at Arthur Andersen (when there was an Arthur Andersen), the company had a strong point of view on employee development and pricey MBAs. It could be summed up as "we've got it covered." Most training happened on the job through successes and rare failures (or shredding mishaps). For more meaty upgrades, the company sent employees to a college campus it owned in St. Charles, Illinois. I was fortunate enough to attend as both a student and instructor. It really was a powerful way to transfer knowledge, bond with colleagues, and definitely never, ever kiss anyone you worked with. At the lower end of the spectrum, the unfairly maligned Hamburger University run by McDonald's helps employees move into management roles with a custom curriculum taught by the company's managers.

Replace Unemployment with a Short-Work Program   Germany was incredibly successful during the recession in no small part because it convinced companies to cut employee work hours instead of firing them. The companies were able to use employee payroll deductions to pay for training during the off days. At its peak, the program had 1.5 million participants. Well done, Germany. I don't see why a program like this couldn't be the norm for companies looking to cut costs. Accelerating attrition instead of casting workers aside isn't the *wurst* idea in the world. (Sorry, I couldn't resist.)

Turn the Unemployed into Entrepreneurs   The Kauffman Foundation, which promotes and sponsors entrepreneurship, created some of the more interesting programs. For example, it partnered with the Michigan Small Business and Technology Center to help the unemployed start new ventures. The program offered recession survival courses to existing businesses and advice and connections to new ones.

Noncelebrity Apprentice

As I write the word "apprentice," it conjures one of two images: an attractive reality show contestant battling to work for a blowhard real estate mogul or a young boy fixing a shoe under the watchful eye of an old, London cobbler, circa 1832. Luckily, there are modern versions of apprenticeship that can help businesses fill sales, medical, and skilled jobs with qualified candidates without a degree.

CVS pharmacy technician apprenticeships are almost as popular in New Jersey as fist-pumping at the Jersey Shore. The program offers high school seniors 2,000 hours of paid on-the-job training, tuition assistance for needed certification courses, mentorship, and job placement with the company. It's a real career that can pay for gym, tan, and laundry.

By the end of 2009, Germany's apprenticeship program kept the country's youth unemployment rate at 8.2 percent while Spain's was at 39 percent. Ten others in the European Union were above 20 percent. In the U.S., that number was over 18 percent, up from 13 percent before the recession. Ahhh, to be young and able to sleep in . . . it could become a lifelong habit. While Germany's program isn't perfect (as all other things are), it plugs hundreds of thousands of students into the job market each year. It's expensive for businesses upfront, but eventually pays off. Even Germany isn't immune to global declines in jobs for humans or occasional imbalances. For example, the system has recently produced a surplus of hairdressers, which explains why Angela Merkel never suffers from bedhead.

Of course, Hollywood talent agencies have a legendary apprenticeship program where everyone starts out in the mailroom and it's extremely competitive. Just goes to show the caliber of people and level of output you can get for very little money when the job or industry is that attractive. Cobblers and accounting firms might want to curb their enthusiasm.

Jóvenes (youth) programs in Latin American countries mandate that employers hire graduating apprentices. What are they, socialists? The government also requires the teaching of life skills in addition to technical ones. Participating businesses are usually small and the programs have not been proven at a larger scale.

So What?

After reading this chapter, I bet you can't wait to run out and buy your little daughter a sander and nail gun. After she builds her own dollhouse, I'll know my work is done. More importantly, if you start, sponsor, or build a school that does any of the things I mentioned, even better. For now, I'll settle for the possibility that I inspired you to think differently about what education can be. In the next chapter, I'll talk about a special brand of makers: micropreneurs. Feeding their needs—or becoming one—might just rescue and redefine our economy.

CHAPTER 7

Liberate Micropreneurs

The burden of growing the U.S. economy will fall almost entirely on libertines who take the risk to start businesses—from restaurants to aviation plants to app development shops. If they self-actualize, they become the employers of tomorrow. Micropreneurship, or the incubation of new businesses, will rescue the U.S. economy. To do it, some will ride the wave of opportunity created by new government incentives; others will have to overcome clunky regulations and unnecessary friction. To give you a sense of what we're up against, let's talk about my second-favorite topic, China. (My first, of course, is American innovation. Pizza and red velvet cake are third and fourth, respectively.)

China is a ridiculously opaque market. From what we know, there are 43 million companies in China that employ 93 percent of Chinese workers, according to the *Economist*. Two-thirds of companies are not majority owned by the state; they produce about 70 percent of the country's gross domestic product. Abundant lending, a tsunami of outside investment, and a sheer hunger for success (and sometimes actual hunger) make China an entrepreneurial juggernaut. It doesn't hurt that the government is willing to make people who cause problems disappear to clear the way for commerce. The kinds of businesses China creates are often capital intensive and ideal for exports and job creation.

According to University of California, Berkeley professor and writer Vivek Wadhwa, between 1992 and 2005 existing businesses destroyed one million jobs per year, while start-ups created three million a year. As you can see in Figure 7.1, new micro start-ups with

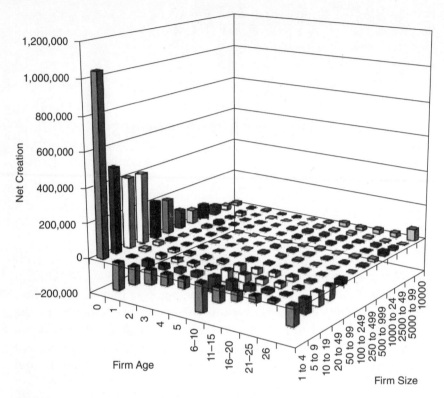

Figure 7.1   Net Job Creation by Firm Age and Size, 1987–2005
Source: U.S. Census Bureau.

four or fewer employees accounted for most of that growth, 20 percent to be exact.

The U.S. has about 6 million companies; 3.6 million of these are micro firms. Few are brash, young programmers with Macbooks, ironic T-shirts, and fistfuls of venture capital. The vast majority are small businesses with humble aspirations funded by bank loans. By 2005, entrepreneurial activity began to stagnate. It wasn't for a lack of good ideas. The biggest obstacles were access to capital, shortage of business skills, and risk aversion. Sure, competent government policies could unleash a torrent of micropreneurship. Good luck waiting for that. Established businesses can fill this void and reap all sorts of rewards by empowering would-be entrepreneurs to save the economy. As for these saviors, they'll have more options than ever. So grab a mug of hot chocolate with mini marshmallows and let's talk about empowering these strivers and saviors of America.

Splice Entrepreneurship into Education

Imagine you were taller, faster, and stronger than any basketball player you've ever played against. You could dunk since you were a zygote. But your parents want you to study accounting. In the NBA, you'd earn millions. At school, you'd learn why no one ever whispers amortization in a girl's ear to get her in the mood. Hundreds of smart, entrepreneurial students find themselves whispering amortization instead of incorporation every year. Michael Dell, Bill Gates, and Larry Ellison never finished college and neither should a select group of others. It's in our collective economic interest to help them get to market sooner and start generating jobs. Some are beginning to pick up on that trend.

Automation can free up resources. Vocational training and apprenticeships can make makers at the lower and midrange of the job scale. Micropreneurship accelerates the super-doers. There is a mass-market opportunity for new types of schools that are linked to business and get private funding. These schools will produce more innovators, engineers, and tinkerers who don't mind getting their hands dirty.

Run Schools like Businesses

Step one is to create flexible, responsive schools that can change curricula quickly without having to pass laws. Charter schools are privately run, but get fees for each student from the state. They can also raise money in other ways, like corporate sponsorships (or even mercenary operations, I suppose). Admission is usually by lottery. Charter schools can teach anything they want as long as kids meet minimum testing standards. They're usually far more successful than public schools. If it gets the job done, they are free to shower teachers with jewels and exotic cheeses. These schools are a great alternative to public education, but their numbers have been artificially capped by government. It's time to unleash their powers and develop ways to choose and monitor the best operators. Eventually, most kids can be migrated to this system. In the long run, charter schools will control costs through innovation and private partnerships, getting government out of the management business, and focused on outcomes.

Create Engineers and Scientists

Microsoft's High School of the Future in a poor Philadelphia neighborhood focuses kids on technology and learning from small failures (Windows Vista?). The school exposes kids to corporations and makes sure they set and achieve the goal of making it to college. Author and futurist Ray Kurzweil started Singularity University to focus on preparing entrepreneurs to advance technology. The school brings in top experts in science to speak (no matter how much some kids beg for Justin Bieber instead).

Mormonize

Econovation is not L. Ron Hubbard's *Dianetics* or Joseph Smith's *Book of Mormon*. I will not send Tom Cruise to convert Oprah or recruit followers in the Congo. I do know a good idea when I see it. To generalize, Mormons are incredibly (and disproportionately) successful at business. Although they're just 2 percent of the population, Mormons hold some of the highest executive positions in companies around the world, according to a June 9, 2011 article in *BusinessWeek* called "God's MBAs." Followers are creative, disciplined, and self-reliant. Some top companies hire as many graduates from Brigham Young University as they do Yale. In fact, BYU spawns more patents and start-ups per $1 of research than any other school. The Mormon Church's wealth is estimated at $30 billion, and in its own quiet way, it's leaving an indelible mark on American business. As important as it is to our future for education to *work with* business, it is even more important to our future to raise leaders and entrepreneurs who *think like* businesses. For that, we could all learn a few things from Mormons.

The Mormon ethic starts early with communication. By the age of three, kids are expected to learn to speak in public forums and teach. Young kids also have community responsibilities that teach discipline and structure. Those skills become essential when, at 19, kids go on two-year missions to remote or undeveloped parts of the world. They must give up perks and live among the people they are trying to convert. Then, it all comes down to selling. Not knowing the language and having little money or no safety net forces these missionaries to get creative. Whether you're selling the idea of Latter Day Saints or a new vacuum cleaner, you need to show results. That's where Mormon leadership skills get developed—creating new ways to attract converts, leading people, and being forced to overcome failures. When they come back, these young adults have effectively run a business and know how to deal with adversity in ways a textbook could never teach.

It's worth overemphasizing: Selling at a very young age is the key to why Mormons are so good at business. All business is sales. When I think back on all the jobs I've ever had, selling computers and electronics at Radio Shack's Tandy Computer Center during college was the most challenging and rewarding. Think selling lots of shiny, powerful Macs for $1,200 is hard? Try getting a lower-middle-class customer to buy an 80-pound behemoth for $2,400 (in 1990s dollars!) that does nothing out of the box but show a black screen with a command prompt—and has no Internet connection! I had no choice but to get good fast; the other salesmen were. Everyone improvised and got others to help out. Even now, I respect those guys more than any PowerPoint wizard I've met since.

Back to Mormons. I bet you can't imagine a suburban mom, who spent two decades protecting her child from everything and making sure they got trophies for the slightest movement, suddenly saying, "Okay, now you're 18, here's your ticket to Korea. Come back with disciples." In some ways, that is exactly what needs to happen, minus the disciples. It's not clear how much of Mormonism's business discipline can be replicated without the religious ethic and upbringing, but one hint lies in another desert far from Utah: Israel. Despite its religious overtones, Israel is a secular country, just like the U.S., with a penchant for entrepreneurialism and innovation. According to Dan Senor, a venture capitalist and *Wall Street Journal* contributor, "Per capita, Israel raises 2.5 times as much venture capital as the U.S., 30 times more than Europe, 80 times more than India, and 350 times more than China."* One of the main differences between the United States and Israel is Israel's mandatory military service:

---

*Start-up Nation: The Story of Israel's Economic Miracle, www.startupnationbook.com.

three years for men and two for women. According to Senor, Israelis learn leadership, discipline, and teamwork in a way others do not. Those exiting service are more mature and ready to take calculated risks and succeed doing so.

Service doesn't have to involve tanks or Torahs to create business leaders. It's beyond the scope of this book to suggest that government needs to mandate military service or public service, but it's my book so I'll write what I want! In all seriousness, I think this entire enterprise can be accomplished through business-sponsored civil service the same way that the GI Bill pays tuition costs for soldiers who serve. Companies could recruit better candidates if they sponsored national service programs structured the same way. These post-high school programs could work exactly the same way as charter schools, except the mission might be to build low-income housing, teach English to immigrants, or even build wells in Tanzania. This can't work like a camp. Programs must require at least a one-year commitment and their style would lie somewhere between Joseph Smith and Netanyahu (Israel's Prime Minister).

Colleges as Incubators

By the time they get to college, teens with entrepreneurial tendencies should be treated a little differently. What if they could also turn a profit by the time they graduate? We're not quite there yet, but schools like Babson and University of Miami are inching closer. First-year students at Babson's School of Entrepreneurship start their own business and work it from idea to dissolution. From selling speakers to flip-flops, there is real money on the line, but it's still business with training wheels. Students at Launch Pad, at The University of Miami, have launched more than 45 start-ups since the program began. Businesses range from raising corals for aquariums to planes that launch satellites.

One of the biggest catalysts of this movement is the Ewing Marion Kauffman Foundation, which has given more than $50 million to fund entrepreneurship programs in 19 universities. They are now expanding outside of business. Purdue is working on new uses for soybeans (presumably they're done using them to impersonate real food). Syracuse students are designing wearable technology. Let's hope someone from Calvin Klein is supervising—I'm not falling for the iHat a second time . . .

These programs could eventually evolve to offer conditional scholarships and links to private financing *during* the school year to offset tuition costs and give companies a first-look opportunity at emerging entrepreneurs and their inventions.

Quit and Earn Instead of Pay to Learn

Peter Thiel, former PayPal CEO and venture capitalist, is not a fan of elite business schools. "Why not create 100 Harvard affiliates?" Thiel asks rhetorically. He knows if there were 100 Harvards, they couldn't keep prices high through scarcity and exclusivity. Plus, the rowing team just wouldn't stand for it. High prices and exclusion led Thiel to set up a program giving 20 kids under 20 years old $100,000 each to drop out of school and start a business. He received more than 400 applications, including 17 from Stanford. And more than 100 people in Thiel's network signed up to be mentors. It's too early to gauge results, but this is one way to liberate young entrepreneurs from the shackles of PowerPoint, and still give them the guide rails and cash to help bring their visions to life.

Gain Access to Capital

It's good to see the President acknowledge the importance of small business to the economy. Though government offers small business loans and other incentives, the programs can be exhausting to navigate. I am optimistic about President Obama's Startup America, a $1 billion federal fund that will match early stage private capital one to one (New York City has a similar Entrepreneurial Fund). It's a simple marriage of two worlds, where both parties do what they do best—one picks investments, the other hands out cash, except this time it's for a good cause. Imagine if all the money spent on two wars was instead spent on starting businesses . . . imagine, indeed.

The big dollars are still in the private sector. U.S. financial markets are awash with cash from the Fed's dollar printing. Banks, venture funds, and wealthy investors are desperate for places to stash their cash. As the number of silly social media URLs dwindles, even venture capitalists will start looking for greener pastures. In a way, funding micropreneurship is like solving for sustainable energy. Each will take a portfolio of solutions that hopefully adds up. The challenge will be to find better financing models that unearth diamonds in the rough, reduce the risk of investing in small business, and provide investors with returns they can brag about at the golf club. Here, I'll only focus on nontraditional ones that don't rely on massive legislative changes or lobbying.

Crowdfunding

For a while, the "wisdom of crowds" was the hottest buzzword (buzz term?) in all the land. Starting around 2006, it came up in every meeting as if it just cured lymphoma. The crowd can be effective at picking winners in the same way democracy can be effective in choosing good leaders. Of course, voting has a tendency to improve when participants have money at stake. Lots of start-ups have sprung up to help businesses of all types attract funding. The only problem is that legally, they can't offer equity. This artificially limits the effectiveness of this channel. Some have started to find ways around that limitation.

Kickstarter is probably the best-known crowdfunding site. It's helped people fund everything from documentaries to glasses that secretly record video. The company is positioned to revolutionize multiple industries from entertainment to publishing to electronics. When people can invest in projects directly, they circumvent official channels that can move like molasses or limit access altogether, like IPOs. Project submitters can offer special deals or exclusives to investors, but not stock. ProFounder inches one step closer to this Holy Grail by allowing start-ups to offer a share of future profits to investors. WebEquity.org is interesting because it allows people to trade their labor for equity in the company. It isn't yet available in the United States, possibly because prison food is not delicious. On paper, Cofundit might have the most compelling approach. This European company offers professional valuation, performance monitoring of all your investments, and most importantly, equity. The company also seeks experts to contribute advice and reviews to various businesses. Ah, free labor. You have to love the Internet.

Crowdmaking

Taking crowdfunding one step further, Quirky not only sources inventions from people, but it runs the end-to-end process from turning an idea into a manufactured product. The company uses its

30,000-member site to vet the ideas that will be most successful and gauge demand before producing the final product. It then shares the profits with the creators. While what the company shares isn't as much as what a well-capitalized inventor would make, Quirky operates on the fringes where, without its help and expertise, the product would never make it to market. This is the kind of model that can unlock the potential of individual inventors and can be scouted by larger companies to hire innovators of the future.

Corporate Funding

Corporations shouldn't shy away from crowdfunding either. Some, like Cisco and Netflix, have run public challenges and offered prizes for winners. In the case of Netflix, it gave away a million dollars to the team that created the most accurate movie recommendation algorithm. It was a cheap way to outsource development of core functionality that could have taken far more time and money. By helping a larger corporation in such a public forum, it's also a great way to give competing micropreneurs the attention and capital they need to help their businesses take off.

I also like Procter & Gamble's model where it simply posts a list of discoveries it wants on its web site. Any business that has that technology or a viable solution can pitch it. In fact, this open procurement approach will shine over the next decade and help create ecosystems of suppliers. New small businesses can emerge built specifically around the needs of these larger corporations with access to new markets and customers. Coupled with better funding mechanisms, the crowd can swarm around the most viable opportunities. In this case, however, the crowd is made up of small businesses.

Attendees at my keynotes often ask me what their son or daughter should study. My advice is to use the big challenges companies are posting on their web sites as a guide for where there will be demand in the future.

Catch and Release

According to UC Berkeley's Vivek Wadhwa, developers who venture out on their own make a larger economic impact than even the cream of the crop that Google attracts. He wonders if Google would be better off liberating them by providing seed funding in exchange for a stake. I'd take that idea in a slightly different direction. Google already invests in lots of companies or buys them outright. The real value is if companies in other industries created formal programs to do this. That way, adventurous employees can develop their businesses outside corporate politics and be considered an investment rather than an expense on the P&L. Many of the most successful start-ups are customer-funded, where the first customer gets more customization and a perpetual license in exchange for being first. Plus, who better to support than your own company's alumni?

Borrowing Better

Equity isn't the only game in town. Some are using social tools to facilitate lending. Lending Club, which up to now, has focused on helping people lend to other people, is planning a move into the small business space. Assuming it can overcome the challenges of getting good information on borrowers and attracting adventurous lenders, it could become an interesting option. Currently, lenders can partially fund people's loans based on their credit score, reason for borrowing, and payment history, among other criteria. Kabbage—another small business lender—isn't quite crowd funded, but it does use information generated from eBay reviews and social media to determine how much it will lend to a given business. The company has closely integrated with eBay's platform and focuses on small online sellers with plans to expand to Amazon and other nonplatform-based businesses.

Can't Forget Uncle $am

The Small Business Administration loan program is one of the ways the U.S. will continue lending out some of the freshest, greenest dollars printed by the Fed. Chase, alone, lent $10 billion to small businesses in 2010. Some of the new programs specifically target exporters, manufacturers, even authors of innovation books (I wish). Several states will continue sponsoring business loan programs.

Missouri's Boost initiative offers government loans of up to $500,000 to small businesses that want to buy land or machinery to expand but do not have good enough credit. Connecticut gave smaller grants of $5,000 to $10,000 to help aerospace manufacturers retool to make medical products. One such company, Habco, used the money to assess the feasibility of a machine to help stroke victims walk again. Not one cent of that money was spent on its "I Can't Believe I Got Cash from the Government"-themed Christmas party.

Close the Confidence and Knowledge Gaps

Digital micropreneurs and those in more traditional, capital-intensive industries approach their knowledge gap in very different ways. Young, fearless digital tycoons live and breathe technology and often know their competitors better than anyone. What they don't know, they can get online at sites like OpenForum, Mashable, or Quora. Their inexperience starts to show in getting senior-level connections to navigate the investor landscape. In many cases, the void has been filled by executives at incubators, networking groups like the Young Entrepreneur Council, or informal school-linked groups like the Columbia Venture Community. Some of the best support networks are also profitable start-ups themselves. FoundersClub is a fee-based service that offers company founders exclusive benefits at top merchants and travel partners. It also provides members access to each other. Having attended one of their events, I have to say, it was invigorating to be in a room filled with so many possibilities and smart, young leaders helping each other succeed. (If that last sentence gets me a free membership, I will be sure to disclose it on my web site, ideafaktory.com). There are no *Econovation* ad placements!

One of the most successful models for entrepreneurs in high-growth industries has been Endeavor.org. This global network started in New York but quickly expanded. It typically establishes itself in high potential, economically stable cities and creates a board of local business leaders to select high potential entrepreneurs. Those selected get access to mentors, talent, and capital. The network estimates that by 2009 its 550-plus member companies had created more than 130,000 high-paying jobs and were generating more than $2.5 billion in annual revenues.

Traditional small businesses have a somewhat different path. They are usually more capital intensive, requiring real estate or equipment. Most don't attract the buzz, cash, or mentorship that tech start-ups get. Owners are often stretched too thin to keep up with the latest trends or best practices. These owners, or prospective owners, tend to be older, somewhat more risk-averse, or uncertain. Amazingly, they're getting high-quality advice from an unlikely source: the U.S. government. Getting help from the government is like having a homeless guy on the train drop *his* change in *your* cup. You start to wonder, "How did things get this bad?" In the coming years, the U.S. will be so desperate for small business growth you might want to get a bigger cup for your next ride.

Traderoots.org is a service from the Department of Commerce that will help domestic producers export. It helps make connections, remove barriers, and even brew a fresh pot of joe for you in the morning. President Obama's National Export Initiative is looking to help small and mid-sized companies export green technologies. The Manufacturing Extension Partnership has more than 1,400 technical experts in every state who help small and midsized manufacturers with "technology acceleration, supplier development, sustainability, workforce and continuous improvement." It also says it generates $32 in new sales for every dollar invested in the program. SCORE StartSMART is another program that provides mentoring and seminars to small business owners on everything from business plans to financing.

In the next decade, the real action will be in states and localities throwing hopeful cash at businesses (possibly from unpaid pensions). Florida's GrowFL program provides free business analysis to help companies find new markets, use social media, or get industry analysis. The program is free for companies with at least $1 million in sales or 10 or more employees. About 100 qualifying companies signed up. North Carolina has a similar program. Line up and don't be afraid to ask, the worst they can say is no.

The Health Albatross

Not only do health care costs keep rising by as much as 30 percent a year, but they might be the single greatest threat to entrepreneurship. If there were ever a case for a single-payer system, it would be based on economic value lost from everyone who remains an employee instead of starting a business. If you're married with kids and want to start a company, you have enough to worry about without the possibility of being bankrupted by a sudden illness in the family. With the insanely partisan debate on health care, it's lobbyists, not sound economics, that win. There is an opportunity here for private alternative models that unlock this pent-up value. One approach could be to swap equity for coverage. Large corporations or even insurers could extend their umbrella insurance to a new business in exchange for a share of ownership, convertible debt, or other bartered perks, like heavily discounted services for the corporation or its employees.

Disneyfication for Micropreneurs

The foundation of any successful new business is its surroundings. The likelihood of the next Disney theme park opening in downtown Detroit is about the same as the next hot dance club opening in Wasilla, Alaska. Of course, both of those are stand-alone businesses. Long-term success on the scale the U.S. needs will rely on intertwined networks of businesses that have access to customers, a matching workforce, infrastructure, and capital. One of the biggest and most successful ecosystems is in Silicon Valley. There, digital talent, VCs, cash, and innovation intertwine. It also doesn't hurt when your customers can be anywhere and all you need to serve them is broadband. Speaking of which, I wrote earlier about Disneyfication, or attracting foreign capital. I believe domestic Disneyfication will be a huge trend that develops local infrastructure, attracts micropreneurs and juices the growth engine.

Ride the New Superhighway

Mayor Bloomberg has diligently inched New York closer to being a more hospitable place for growing a business. Sure, the city has natural advantages in terms of colleges, wealthy taxpayers, and global cultural attractions. It can also be a place that fights change with thousands of competing interest groups. After all, it's a place where some apartments that could rent for $8,000 a month are only able to charge $550 because of rent control. One change most can agree on is building the superhighway of the future, or broadband access. As part of his broader digital plan, the Mayor announced in 2011 that every city park will now have free Wi-Fi through a partnership with AT&T. For the company, the free access points act as a gateway drug to the rest of the company's ubiquitous network.

The New York initiative will become the norm. Almost every city will look to deploy affordable wireless broadband. Once everyone is wired, all kinds of new business services, apps, and revenue possibilities open up. Some people might not even need phones to communicate. In many parts of the city, they could just use an iPod Touch or some other Wi-Fi device. Location services and games will open up to more people. A market for low-cost devices for kids or the poor will also expand.

Build Supplier Ecosystems

Earlier, I wrote about creating bundles around an anchor product or service to attract foreign capital. The same logic could apply for building the next generation of successful small businesses. The key is finding behemoths that are growing and figuring out (or even asking them in a presale scenario) what they want. For example, big companies like Apple, Intel, and Motorola (now Google) will expand as demand for their devices grows. Depending on the nature of that expansion, small businesses can sprout up around these new and emerging needs. While some of these needs might be digital, like new software for Intel engineers to track their research projects, locating small businesses near Intel will allow for constant collaboration that can lead to even more opportunities.

Get Creative with Surplus Real Estate

This country is eyeball deep in excess real estate. Everything got so frothy and overbuilt that private and public property owners will need to think of creative ways to deploy that slack capacity. One way to do it is to help foster small business growth.

Walking through New York City, you'll notice more and more "for rent" signs. It has shades of the early 1980s when huge parts of Manhattan were a wasteland of criminals, empty buildings, and full porn shops. As the real estate bubble deflates, few will buy property. Even with commercial rents falling, there's an undercurrent of entrepreneurship. People want to start businesses, especially in high traffic places like Manhattan, but are not able or willing to pay the high rent. A possible solution is equity-based leasing, where risk is shared between the entrepreneur and the property owner.

For this to work, the landlord has to give up the dream that someone's going to pay $10,000 a month for a shoebox. One option is to cut the price to the bone on a short-term lease and raise it later, if the business survives. A more dynamic approach might be to forego a small, but steady stream of rental income and enter into a revenue-sharing or equity deal with the tenant. If the business succeeds, this extra upside might prove to be a wise bet.

To make this work would require periodic revenue verification, which can be challenging with cash businesses, less so with chains. (Verification could be done by a third party like a bank, a property management company, or an audit firm.) Most importantly, this requires a leap of faith on both sides. Ultimately, an unoccupied space has no upside and it creates a damaging halo-effect on the rest of the community. So which is the real risk?

This idea may also be applied to residential real estate. In fact, individual income is much easier to verify. Of course, your landlord taking a cut of your paycheck would feel a lot like marriage . . . and for most, one spouse is plenty.

There are many other ways to repurpose excess real estate or abandoned communities. Some have suggested converting them to farms to reduce the need for food stamps or developing them into recreational facilities. One idea in particular intrigued me—giving abandoned housing away to immigrants. Mayor Bloomberg believes we could offer amnesty to illegal immigrants in exchange for them committing to live in and hopefully revitalize cities like Detroit with shrinking populations and vast swaths of empty houses. At the high end, we could use that excess capacity to attract immigrants from other parts of the world who could settle here and open doctors' offices, shops, or other small businesses. Countless statistics show that immigrants from India and China are extremely likely to be entrepreneurial and generate jobs.

So What?

All businesses are cogs in a massive supply chain. In the United States, the chain broke down. Young U.S. companies know how to sell services, make web sites, and sell imported goods. By all means, they should continue. To start making the kinds of things a French or Taiwanese company can sell, they'll need capital and know-how. The next generation of entrepreneurs must dare to do more, take bigger risks, and aim for the meaty, gritty part of the innovation spectrum. Luckily, they won't have to do it alone. There are more tools and channels than ever to help good ideas, people, and money find each other. Just like fixing education is everyone's problem, so is helping micropreneurs, libertines, and risk-takers flourish. Whenever someone I know starts a company, I find myself going out of my way to help them—with ideas, introductions, and occasionally, an investment. Many others do the same. There is something brave and admirable about those who overcome the natural fear of failure to start a business. Everyone from family members to employees of megacorporations has an important role to play in making micro-preneurs' risks pay off. We all have a stake in their success.

In the next and final chapter, we go deep into the gears of our domestic machine and talk about using micro levers (like pricing and incentives) to capitalize on macro trends, especially when it comes to selling in a saturated market.

CHAPTER

Build an "Incentive Nation"

When was the last time you dragged a big, plastic bag full of empty bottles and cans to your supermarket and demanded your deposits back? When New York first introduced its $.05 deposit law, beverage companies fought it. Consumers resented paying more for their corn syrup fix. Kids, however, loved it. It was the only way to make money that wouldn't lead to our parents being arrested for child labor violations. Over time, the process improved. Recycling machines replaced clueless clerks, who did more recounts than the Florida election bureau. By the time I discovered girls, I learned collecting bottles was not an aphrodisiac. I began treating the deposit as a tax, but my habit of recycling stuck. I was not alone. States with these programs have 64 percent less roadside litter and bottle recycling rates of 70 percent, compared to 33 percent for other states. The system also created enough economic incentive for companies like Pepsi and Waste Management to innovate new machines and business models, like the ecoATM that donates deposit money to charity.

The next decade will be a transitional one for the United States. With government and people recovering from a near-fatal bout with consumerism, a return to "producerism" won't happen all at once. In the meantime, people will continue shopping, just not at self-destructive levels, That leaves lots of retail and service businesses competing for a shrinking pie. Microeconomic tools like pricing and incentives hold the key to motivating the emerging maker to consume . . . at your business.

I define an incentive as the minimum reward needed to encourage or discourage a behavior. That last part can also be called a penalty or disincentive (an awful word I'm sure a consultant or Lord Voldemort invented). That reward does not have to be cash. In fact, some of the most rewarding payments over the next decade will be made in Facebook likes, badges, and wampum. Incentive Nation is all about finding new ways to wield pricing like a bootleg Kit Kat at a fat camp. In a maker economy, motivation and inspiration will fuel consumption, not debt.

Touched by the Hand of Go . . . vernment

I'll do my best to resist diving into the bottomless pit of misguided government incentives. I'll cover those in a future version of *Econovation* for government, institutions, and the people who love them. The government does offer a few great examples of how pricing distorts individual behavior. Many little actions snowball into macro-level imbalances, deficits, and profits. Consider the following ways government incentives did just that. They're also building blocks for the next wave of *Econovation* opportunities.

Pay per Procedure

One of the most broken parts of our health care system is that it reimburses based on each procedure performed. Conduct more procedures, make more money. That caused a proliferation of unnecessary testing, referral kickbacks among doctors, and a spiraling cost structure. This incentive scheme triggered an explosion of innovation in the number of tests available and gave consumers infinite ways to be drained of blood, urine, and cash. So far, new health care reform does not address this issue, creating an opportunity for providers and companies to reprice their systems to be based on outcomes, not inputs.

The worst part of this is that health care pricing doesn't create enough counterbalancing friction on the patient's side. Patients need to bear more of the per-use cost of each procedure, test, and visit. That friction would reduce overutilization of procedures throughout the system. It's the same thing that keeps non-fans out of concerts that charge $30, but causes them to flock if it's free. Paying for every sip of water and for electricity is what makes you yell at your kids when they leave the lights on or water running, at least until Child Protective Services or Oprah shows up. Consumption taxes can be a powerful way to fix these systemic problems.

Financial Services Risks and Wages

The financial crisis is like a kaleidoscope; everyone sees something different and illuminating. I choose to look at it through the lens of bad incentives. When the government (through Fannie and Freddie) guaranteed every sketchy mortgage, lenders had no incentive to manage risk—and they didn't. This endless stream of phony loans created a surplus of high-paying jobs in finance, an industry that produces nothing you could live in, eat, or wear. Big money meant top talent was creating spreadsheets, not curing cancer; revolutionizing transportation; or breeding boneless, ready-to-eat chickens. With the government moving to drive exports, fresh new wage distortions await in energy, tech, and manufacturing. Later, I'll talk about how these new misalignments will again remake the labor market and require new kinds of incentives.

Green. Solved. Really.

No matter how many hipsters or pseudo-revolutionaries with Che Guevara tattoos buy (or steal) Chevy Volts, voluntary greenness doesn't scale like higher prices do. When I first saw the numbers in Figure 8.1, they moved me almost as much as a gutsy performance by Reese Witherspoon. As gas prices rise, people buy less of everything. They literally stop leaving the house. Now that's what I call green. Unfortunately, in a country fueled entirely by consumption, that's also economic suicide. If price isn't a powerful lever, I don't know what is.

Like a bad action movie whose entire plot could be cleared up with just one phone call, the U.S. fuel strategy could easily star Chris Tucker and Jackie Chan. Instead of taxing foreign oil consumption to upgrade to a sustainable infrastructure, the United States subsidizes oil companies. That math is about to change. A dollar decline, foreign fuel lust, and our own export surge will finally make fuel alternatives viable. It will also attract government R&D subsidies. Low-income consumers will quickly respond by adjusting how they live and commute. At the more elastic end of the curve, gas would

Figure 8.1   Price of Gasoline versus Percentage Change in National Retail Sales (excluding Auto and Gas)

Source: U.S. Federal Reserve.

have to cost $375 per gallon to keep Lebron James out of his Hummer.

Price, Love, and Understanding

When it comes to pricing and incentives, it's about mastering how behaviors will affect long-term economic viability. Many businesses need to master the economics of motivation—internally and externally.

Incentivize Obsolescence, Kill Zombies

The most prominent feature of the coming decade is uncertainty and change. In cases where we can control it, change will be incredibly powerful and liberating. It will create the next Internet or, at least, the next Barney craze. When someone else drives the change bus, companies and individuals will see currency fluctuations, price volatility, and the ripple effects of indebtedness. Everything from job security to technology will be in flux. Just as individuals move from the permanence of owning to the transience of renting, companies need to weave flexibility into how they do things. That's no easy task.

Business gurus talk about change, but every inclination of every organization—and person in it—is to nest. The older the company, the more complex and embedded its systems, rules, and habits become. It attacks change with antibodies, like it's an invading virus. Real change often comes too late—long after complexity has ground the gears to a halt. One of the most common misconceptions is that companies don't do enough of the right things. The bigger problem is they don't *stop* doing enough of the wrong ones.

From futuristic robots to government agencies, once something is created, its Darwinistic purpose is to survive. Rarely do useless laws or ineffective agencies get decommissioned. More often, a new agency is created, like the Department of Homeland Security, and layered on top of others. In business, once you create a department, product, or job role, entire ecosystems build up around them. Employees depend on those jobs for their children's tuition; leaders fear losing power and leverage; suppliers have a customer they want to keep forever. I've known companies where entire product lines generate less revenue than the salaries of the people running them, but they continue to exist. I'm not sure how long it took to decommission AOL's CD shipping department or to phase out book and newspaper printing departments, but few formal processes exist to do so. When social media becomes just another tool in the marketing tool kit, who will break the news to the SVP of Social Media?

Because business zombies rarely die of natural causes, it's important to create a system that incentivizes killing them before they start snacking on your company's flesh.

Stay Broad

The most basic tactic is not to create narrow job definitions or hire people with niche, nonadaptable skills. Kevin Rose, founder of Digg.com, admits that his biggest mistake was hiring good programmers who knew how to code in a certain language instead of hiring really smart people who can adapt and learn anything as circumstances and technologies changed.

Separate Powers

Innovation can produce big winners and losers, with zombies in between. One of the most successful ways to prevent zombies from lingering is to separate the funding and the management of the process. An independent committee can approve the larger projects at scheduled checkpoints, as long as its members have as much to gain from successful projects outside their businesses as they do from those they manage. In a committee model, members have to abstain from voting on projects in their own business. A secret ballot couldn't hurt, either.

Mandate Obsolescence

Why leave anything to chance? Companies should flip the conversation entirely. The debate about shutting something down needs to be flushed out of the deep, dark corners of the boardroom. Why not start every new project, job, or business with the idea that once it reaches its stated goal or duration, it gets dissolved, like a task force?

Alternatively, if performance sinks below a minimum share, sales, or profit threshold, it gets placed on a watch list. How long anything stays on the list will depend on the industry, but the expectation is that at some point, it will be killed if things don't change. Knowing that an obsolescence mandate exists from the start will create a natural incentive to innovate. For this to work, companies need a consistent way to transition workers into their next role and decommission assets without people panicking about losing their jobs.

Instill a Long-Term Bias

It's common to choose to fund a low-risk marketing campaign instead of a new development project, like a bed with a refrigerated snack drawer. Sometimes, it's the right decision. Over time, making too many short-term trade-offs could mean bankruptcy, or worse, '70s furniture. Mature markets like the United States and categories like furniture and cereal demand a long-term bias. A furniture company's future might rely more on multiyear investments like emerging markets, R&D, and technology platforms than on good design, zero-percent financing, or free mattress covers. There are some obvious and obscure places to look for these impurities and ways to exorcise them. Here are three examples:

1. **The obvious:** One of the biggest pressures at big, public companies is doting over quarterly financials like a helicopter mom showing up with cookies at her daughter's dorm during finals week. One company that rebelled was Unilever, pumping extra money into R&D to build its innovation pipeline. It also stopped reporting quarterly profits and issuing guidance to analysts. (Hmm, I wonder if anything bad would ever happen to the economy if analysts weren't as accurate. Unilever concluded that it doesn't run on a 90-day cycle and neither should its reporting. The stock took a short-term hit but was up 35 percent two years later.

2. **The prospective:** Stock options, long-term vesting, and multiyear bonuses are some of the ways companies bake in a long-term perspective. There are others. Pipeline metrics can help. In the early stages, that means how much of your budget you're plowing into new growth opportunities. As you move down the pipeline, milestone metrics should say how quickly you're getting new capabilities into the market. Once new things are launched, it's about measuring adoption rates to gauge viability as Google does. Finally, there's the question of how much of your revenue comes from new business, markets, or customers. New colors of laptops would not count as a new business if you were Dell. A new cloud service would. Another good behavior metric is linking bonuses across departments. If 25 percent of your bonus is tied to the performance of another division, it forces collaboration in ways team-building exercises and a room full of stress balls never could.

3. **The obscure:** The *American Idol* competition lasts several months. During that time, contestants might get a voice coach or gargle with baking soda, but they're not likely to enroll in a music school to learn songwriting or guitar. It's the same at many companies. Senior leaders may have long-term incentives, but the middle- and junior-level employees didn't get that memo. For example, at companies with frequent job rotations, people only stay in a role for 12 to 24 months. That's 6 months of ramp-up, 6 to 12 months of peak performance, and the rest interviewing for their next role or promotion. To them, anything with a one-year build and a two-year payoff is kryptonite. One way to change that is by deemphasizing revenue metrics for junior (nonsales) positions, focusing

more on milestones. Another more complicated way is to make people want to stay longer by flattening the organization. Broader jobs make for more challenging roles. After all, renters don't install marble tiles in their bathrooms.

Master Micro Incentives vs. Macro Consequences

Remember how exciting it was to discover Nabisco's Snackwells low-fat cookies back in the 1990s? I could eat the entire box. I did eat the entire box. Over and over again. Each time, I consumed more calories than if I had a few Chips Ahoy cookies. The same thing happened with energy efficiency. It's called the rebound effect. The *New York Times* ran an article about government efficiency standards imposed on washing machines and cars.* By saving water and energy, washing machines became less effective. People had to wash things more frequently, wasting even more energy. Car manufacturers also had to make compromises by making cars lighter. The thin materials couldn't handle impact very well, converting good intentions into rolling roulette. Should I even bother describing the problem with low-flow toilets?

More than 500 studies have shown that increasing manufacturing efficiency is almost never green. Instead, more products can be pumped out faster. You achieve savings per unit, but never in aggregate. Consumers simply redirect money saved by efficiencies toward other purchases that make penguins sweat. Taxes are a far more effective mechanism, but they scare politicians much more than scores of dead penguins. Raising price reduces aggregate consumption because people buy less and manufacturers make less. So if the intent is to make things green, only consumption tax accomplishes the intended goal.

Companies are in business to increase aggregate demand, not reduce it. They want new customers, more frequent visits, and bigger purchases. One emerging trend most businesses think is helping might be doing the exact opposite. Coupons and deals are everywhere. I even bought a Groupon to visit my parents for four hours, but I only need to stay for two. Rising food prices, mobile technology, and a rocky economy conditioned people to look for coupons

---

*"When Energy Efficiency Sullies the Environment," *New York Times*, www.nytimes .com/2011/03/08/science/08tier.html.

to buy anything. Otherwise, they'll postpone buying. The success of individual deal campaigns can mask losses from delayers and shrink long-term profitability. This can be especially damaging to small businesses that already have narrow margins and might be teetering on desperation when they give away their services at a loss through a deal site. A less dire effect of deep or frequent discounts is they can hurt perception of quality and intent to buy, especially for established brands. In some cases, companies would be better off just running a sale. Time limitations and single-item focus of many deal sites makes it hard to sell profitable add-ons and upgrades. However, steep discounts from unknowns like Scrapple Computer, Bulgaree Jewels, and Jessie's Grill can tempt a customer to experiment.

Deals will trigger two other macro consequences. They create a wealth transfer from manufacturers and retailers to outside marketers, middlemen, and ad firms that serve up offers. This is similar to what insurers did in health care, precipitating higher prices by adding a layer between the buyer and seller. For consumers, deal sites like Groupon and LivingSocial raise overall consumption using deal psychology to create purchases, because a deal seems too good to be true. Same as the Snackwells cookies.

One example of a company that has avoided coupon conditioning is Trader Joe's. This successful supermarket chain is a fraction of the size of typical supermarkets. It never runs sales or offers discounts in a category known for constant sales or those sad-looking four-color circulars. Without tweets and Badges, why is every Trader Joe's packed? Its secret is partnering with manufacturers to create high-quality, exclusive items. Most of what's sold in the store is the house brand. No reason to discount when no one else sells the same thing. You might find a different brand's spicy hummus for less, but customers are conditioned to expect a consistently fair price for their overall basket of goods. Instead of promoting individual values, Trader Joe's wants to *be the value.*

Mind Your Elasticity

Price elasticity determines how much you can raise prices before customers stop buying, look for alternatives, or throw bricks through your windows (as some did in Asia when rice prices skyrocketed). Understanding your company's pricing flexibility will become more important as three macro pressures mount:

1. Rising commodity prices will mandate frequent adaptation.
2. The expense of complying with new regulations, especially for finance companies and telcos.
3. The need for new tax revenues.

Because some of the biggest and most profitable companies hardly pay any taxes, political pressure will paint a target on them (and on their Bermuda shell companies). The inevitable question will be: Eat it or pass it on? When Congress fired its first shot by lowering debit card fees, banks immediately dropped debit rewards and added a new fee for each time you think about your money.

Consider the following three things in terms of how macro conditions will affect the price you can charge.

1. **Who is buying?** Most companies know who buys their products or at least which celebrity they'd like to see wear it on the red carpet. There are many variables that go into the complex stew of what someone will pay for a product. After the recession, it became clear that buying habits are more about how safe, rich, or secure people *feel* than how much they have in the bank. Feeling rich and confident about the future sells both small indulgences and big boats. Uncertainty can even make millionaires abandon that daily caramel macchiato when it breaks $5. In 2010, Fidelity Investments found that 42 percent of millionaires did not feel wealthy. That's down from 46 percent in 2009, but still substantial. This group felt it needed at least $7.5 million in investable assets to feel rich. By comparison, the average household net worth is $120,000 including real estate. What's sadder than a millionaire downgrading to Bounty Basic?
2. **How essential is it?** Even though President Obama promised to raise the cost of wireless spectrum, and local governments plan to increase mobile taxes, wireless companies are unfazed. The phone is more of a limb than a product these days. Most utility prices are fairly elastic, even at the low end. People could sit by candlelight telling ghost stories, but they're likely to give up travel before they give up *Dancing with the Stars*. Gyms could raise prices on hardcore patrons, but casual ones might instead run in the park, do push-ups at home, or go back to bonbons. However, gyms also have untapped ways to

drive higher perceptions of necessity by providing broader health care services or insurance discounts for attending. Concerts and other recreational activities will increasingly compete with cheaper, home-based alternatives. Die-hard fans will always want to see Mick and Keith one last time before they're embalmed. The rest might just download "Start Me Up" from Amazon and listen in the dark, imagining what it would be like to be Mick's drinking buddy or fourth wife.

3. **What are the alternatives?** The number of competitors, margins, and entry barriers are among the best ways to judge competitiveness. Generally, the more competitors, the less pricing power any one player will have. Obscenely high margins mean that somewhere there's a company salivating to come in and disrupt. The decision to enter will be influenced by entry barriers. Three of the most powerful barriers are regulations (financial services), infrastructure (airlines), and networks (credit card networks).

No industry demonstrates the dynamics of all three of these like mobile. Telecoms are heavily regulated and targeted by local governments for tax hikes. But because there are so few competitors with broad coverage and good data networks, they can pass most increases on to consumers. Platform owners like Apple and Google also have pricing power because they have few competitors and they have successful networks of developers, consumers, and manufacturers. When Apple imposed an in-app billing system, it mandated all apps comply with its 30 percent commission structure. Many did. On the extreme end are app makers. Anyone can make one. Sure, some could charge $5.99 instead of $.99, but most compete with 30 or more alternatives in their category. That fragmentation gives them less pricing power and even less bargaining power with platform owners. Even the most dominant players are not immune from mutiny. When Microsoft's fees and terms for Windows got too onerous, IT departments and manufacturers like Dell started experimenting with the open source Linux operating system. Microsoft had to concede.

In the next decade, the U.S. market will be tight and the battle for growth will attract unlikely competitors into new categories. Some will crank up lobbying to help enter businesses historically protected by high margins and regulatory costs. Macro trends and policies will help stir things up. Motivated by aging baby boomers and government insurance coverage for millions of uninsured, companies like Wal-Mart, Walgreens, or even health clubs like Crunch will march deeper into health care. Many Wal-Marts already have independent clinics and offer affordable, generic medicines, but the company has barely scratched the surface. It's just a matter of time before it makes a push into health insurance, negotiating hospital rates, and doing to the medical supply chain what it did to retail.

New players will also be drawn to green energy. As soon as cab companies or other big fleets convert to electric, don't be surprised to see electric charging stations in Costco parking lots or freshly charged batteries offered with your McDonald's Happy Meal.

Financial services are already seeing upheaval. Fat margins and inefficient delivery have attracted telcos (Isis Consortium) and Google (Sprint-Citi-MasterCard partnership) to the mobile payments business and others into banking (SmartyPig) and small business financing (Receivables Exchange).

Maximize Pricing Power   So, what are some ways companies can test the limits of elasticity and maximize pricing power? Some, like mobile service providers and PC manufacturers, have been known to leak preliminary pricing and features to blogs and then evaluate public reaction. If they didn't like the reaction or detected a customer mutiny, they disassociated from the "rumors." Playing out pricing decisions in public can be effective, but it's risky for an established brand. It's like a U.S. senator seeking treatment on *Celebrity Rehab*.

A better way is to create an environment to test and measure different pricing models in select stores, limited online populations, or for certain models. For years, credit card companies have had the ability to run simulated offers to select groups of customers to gauge likely response to a bigger mail campaign (yes, *mail!*). Some retailers set up test stores and observe shoppers in their natural habitat to see how they react to price changes.

To make the whole thing work, two types of data can offer clues about how far your offerings can stretch at higher prices:

1. Track aggregate purchases during different economic scenarios (nationally and regionally).

2. Track individual customer habits over time versus your own or competitors' price changes and sales.

For commodity and many big-ticket purchases, consistency will beat lumpiness. As people do more active budgeting, the cost of fuel, food, rent, clothing, and travel will be scrutinized and compared more than ever. Better hedging of costs can give you a competitive edge as can self-cannibalization (no, not a horror flick) by offering cheaper options that make sense to both parties. One example would be if CVS offered bigger discounts or more loyalty points to use self-checkout instead of a cashier.

Hire Psychologists not MBAs

In the 1930s, the term "Depression era mentality" was coined. People were so shell-shocked by losing everything, they hoarded and saved long after the economy recovered. To a lesser extent, that happened after the Great Recession. Many have different views on shopping, home ownership, and financial security. That calls for psychologists and human behavior experts, not cookie cutter MBAs with spreadsheets, to determine pricing strategy. It's not price that changes behavior, but perceptions of value or even size. Ending prices with 9 or 99 is the old workhorse of psychological pricing, but its exact effect wasn't known until 1996 when a study by Robert Schindler and Thomas Kibarian showed it didn't cause people to buy something, but it did make them spend more.

Price points are another psychological technique retailers and consumer packaged goods (CPG) companies can use. People set psychological thresholds of what certain items should cost and companies do their best to hit those marks. Large CPG companies have used package design to mask price inflation. Instead of breaking a $2.99 price point for an 8-oz. can of tuna, they shrink the package to 6 oz., then 5, until eventually, you need a second can to make grandma's secret recipe. At some point, increasing commodity prices will test the laws of physics. No one wants to live in a world where toilet paper is narrower than dental floss. New approaches will be needed before quality compromises destroy trust and brand perception. Companies are trying alternatives. Breyers started using a natural filler/preservative called Tara gum to make its ice cream.

Pharmacy Duane Reade introduced a line of Delish house brand items at price points that established brands used to occupy.

Behavioral Bribery

There's a new kid on the psychological pricing block. This little trickster bribes people to get his way. At its core, behavioral bribery is an explicit trade. A business gets a quantifiable benefit in exchange for giving the consumer a reward based on perceived value. It's brilliant and insidious. It capitalizes on three trends: glitches in human psychology, stagnating incomes, and the rising costs of certain goods and services. It also spotlights how much bargaining power corporations have in reserve. Consider these ways in which companies put behavioral bribery to work.

Green Guilt   The cheapest thing a company can trade in exchange for customers saving it money is good feelings. One example we've all experienced is the long, impassioned ecological plea in hotels explaining how they'll wash your used towels as long as you understand that will destroy the earth. Leave those towels on the floor at your own (and the planet's) peril. We've seen similar green messages on every bill you get in the mail: "Save trees; paperlessness is next to Godliness." Even manufacturers tell you how green their new product is—as long as you buy it *now*. Go ahead, throw out that old clunker, fridge, or washing machine. That won't produce any waste. At its core, consumption is not green, no matter how green the product. The greenest smartphone is one you keep for four years instead of one; it's not the one made of feathers, compost, and corn flakes. In some cases, these messages do work, but they are most effective when a genuine business case is behind the feel-good message.

In the coming years, there will be real green incentives—both financial and emotional—that will change people's behavior. One is transportation, and by that, I mean not using any. As jobs get more digital and networking technologies improve, *not* traveling to work will be the greenest thing to do. And, many companies will encourage it, as long as they can still eke out good performance. That will decrease real estate costs and create an opportunity to create small workspaces in residential areas. Virtual offices, Starbucks offices, or rewiring public spaces can serve green, gainfully employed homebodies.

Brazil has shown how far green guilt incentives can go by creating Banco Cyan—a bank for water. When you open an account, just like with a regular bank, it begins tracking your water usage. When you use less than your average, you earn points that can be redeemed for water or other consumables at participating vendors. Similar incentives could be offered to recycle, drive less, or use fewer sporks at Kentucky Fried Chicken.

Conditional Cash   Many companies now offer on-site diet programs, health screening, even full blood work. I hardly have time to work; I'm so busy being poked and pricked (by needles). On-site wellness is one way companies try to reduce health care liabilities. Vicodin in the snack machines and fish-oil-laced drinking fountains can't be far behind. The U.K. government paid citizens to lose weight and stop smoking. Scotland offered low-income pregnant women $19.50 a week to stop smoking. After one month, about 60 percent did. (No word on how many started just so they could quit.) In Kent, England, people got 425 pounds if they hit their target weight and kept it off for 24 months. With health costs skyrocketing, larger companies could explore similar incentives.

Brazil, Mexico, and other emerging countries have even more ambitious programs for the poor. They pay women to keep their kids in school, get checkups, and learn about nutrition and disease prevention. Access to family planning is also being introduced. (Something the United States might have to consider as jobs and resources become scarcer.)

Wage Cage   Many companies conduct a *Sophie's Choice*-style compensation survey where employees choose what incentives they value most. The goal is to lower overall costs while retaining top-rated choices like salary and air conditioning. In Washington D.C., compensation trade-offs took on a different flavor. Michelle Rhee, the school chancellor, created two pay plans for teachers—one with lower pay with tenure and another that pays as much as $40,000 more, but the district retains the right to fire them and take away seniority. This is a brilliantly devious workaround for an extremely broken education system. Instead of fighting tenure, it withers it away through economic bribery.

Behavioral bribery cuts both ways. If done wrong, it can have the opposite effect or, at best, be an expensive placebo. A misconception in compensation is that stock options motivate long-term performance. According to a Wharton School study, stock options don't make people work harder. It's only when people make money from their stock options that they feel obligated to perform . . . or at least stop stealing stationery.

Pricing and Incentive Models with a Future

So what kind of models will work in the age of empowered corporations, price-sensitive consumers and emerging global customers? The following are a few worth exploring.

Microsize

As the U.S. economy turns digital, some of Microsoft's and Beyonce's best work is being downloaded illegally around the world. In the United States, the convenient new services have won over many pirates. Often, services like iTunes and Spotify offer the same convenience, but fail to make a dent in piracy. High unemployment in Europe and low relative wages in emerging markets still makes a $1-song and a $3-movie a luxury worth pirating. Legal efforts can help, but they're inefficient, weak, and far from sustainable. Nothing illustrates this point better than the story of Russia's AllofMP3.com. In the mid-2000s, the site amassed a huge global customer base by selling every type of music in every format imaginable for $1 to $3 an album. This was all done with an elegant interface and convenient payment options. The problem? They didn't license any of the music. Everything was pirated. At first, the Russian government resisted, but legal crackdowns and bans by Visa and MasterCard eventually shuttered the site. Its customers were sent back into the arms of BitTorrent and other piracy tools, instead of slowly being converted into legitimate consumers. Shortsighted.

Whatever they lose in margin, companies selling digital goods in emerging markets need to make up in volume, value tiers, and add-ons. The difference between a $.50 movie and one that costs $3 will determine if Hu Chee Kuo is a mild-mannered taxi driver or a master criminal with a soft spot for Jack Black. Low pricing on digital goods can eliminate most of the capital consumed by unproductive legal battles and IP enforcement. This applies to online web services, software, and anything with no marginal cost. Extra copies of Adobe Photoshop or the new Jonas Brothers album cost nothing other than bandwidth.

In the U.S., Apple's iTunes Store is the best example of little purchases adding up. Decoupling songs from albums was the first step. At $0.99, each purchase is so tiny, it hardly warrants any attention. That simplicity eliminated much of the friction previously associated with music purchases. That logic proliferated. New app stores by Amazon, Microsoft, and others feature that same low price, high-volume logic.

High prices try to create scarcity for things that by their nature are abundant. One way to do that is to control access. Clean water is free (or cheap) across the United States. When you go to the airport, security separates you from this abundant thirst quencher. Once you're inside, vendors try to resell you the same Poland Spring for 10 times its cost. Similarly, telcos could block or cripple illegal services, but pirates are motivated and many governments are not. That is why content creators are moving to streaming and web-based services. They offer much more pricing flexibility than downloads or installable software. Warner Bros. even launched a video on-demand service in China in hopes of stemming piracy. In the case of software, web services make it much cheaper to price for low-volume businesses, because there's only one installation to manage, not thousands of tiny ones on different hardware.

Disguise B2B as B2C

Many businesses got used to confident consumers handing them credit cards still warm from terminal friction. With the card taking a siesta, there are ways companies can adapt. One is to disguise a business service as a consumer one. Everyone has a Gmail, Yahoo!, or Hotmail account, but few consider why something so useful costs nothing. It's because you are not the customer. You are a user. Corporations and small businesses that place eerily relevant ads next to your e-mail are the real customers. Ever notice there's no customer service number to call if you have a problem with your account? The real customers can call 1-866-2Google. Simply put, you traded mindshare and privacy to get free email. At least it wasn't a kidney—or your freedom. (Ironically, politics and media work the same way. Big campaign contributors have access to politicians, not lowly voters. Who is really the customer?) All media—radio, TV, Facebook, and deal sites—are B2B businesses that work this way. Even Ticketmaster, which takes a cut from 80 percent of the tickets sold in this country, is a B2B company whose clients are concert venues. The success of all of these businesses relies on deep-pocketed business customers and the reality that people are far more attached to their money than their time or privacy.

Subsidize the Price

When revenue from business sponsors can't support the economics of the service, what it can provide is a subsidy that lowers the cost and increases the number of customers willing to buy. This approach works both online and for physical goods.

Cheaper Hardware   Ever buy a Dell computer and find dozens of supposedly free programs preinstalled? If you've tried to run any of them, you quickly realized most are useless trial versions. Those companies paid Dell a fee that ultimately subsidized the cost of the computer. You paid with awareness and inconvenience to uninstall them. This approach was so successful, HP, Lenovo, and others quickly followed suit. At some point, there was a consumer backlash and Dell started offering some models with a clean install option for a higher price. Others have tried to extend subsidies to make products like computers entirely free, but sponsorships have their limits when it comes to expensive hardware. Cell phone companies regularly subsidize the price of expensive phones in exchange for being repaid over the course of a contract. It's been a successful model, but long-term contracts and termination fees have that air of subjugation that can make consumers bitter and resentful toward your brand. Subsidies can also go horribly wrong as it did when a car rental company tried to offer free rentals that had advertising plastered all over them like race cars. I'm glad to see we're not that desperate yet.

In a way, the difficulty of fully subsidizing physical goods with software or IP–based services is a microcosm for the sad state of U.S. trade. Software and ads produced here have a hard time paying for phones and computers made abroad.

Purchase or Installation Path Access   Have you tried configuring a laptop online? Sometimes you don't get to basics like memory and battery options until you've been forced to consider what software to buy. Getting you to sift through that list is subsidized by the software developers. Similarly, travel booking companies offer insurance upgrades during checkout. Usually the featured provider pays what amounts to rent and a commission to be in that prime spot before checkout. It works the same way when you install software. Winamp, a popular PC media player, always features three to five offers during its installation process. If you are in a rush and don't uncheck the boxes, you might reboot to a new search engine, music site subscription, and a toolbar or two. In the analog world, when you take that guided tour of Chichen Itza pyramids in Mexico and the bus stops at that random empty restaurant or gift shop, those stores pay for that privilege. What's in your installation path?

Subsidize Anything   TrialPay has an interesting model. It turns any product into a currency. Want that new version of QuickBooks? You can pay cash or click on the TrialPay button and sign up for new cell phone service or a membership to Crunch gym and they'll give you QuickBooks for free.

Secondary Product Subsidizes the Primary   Ever wonder why popcorn costs so much at the movies? Each kernel is priced like a college credit. The reason is that the secondary product (concessions) subsidizes the primary one (movies). Only 20 percent of theater revenues come from goodies like Twizzlers and soda, but they represent 40 percent of the profits. The movie is practically the loss leader that gets you through the door, just like eggs, milk, and orange juice do at the supermarket.

Share Your Subsidy   Like many deals sites, Mypoints.com makes money from commissions on items advertised on the site. It also offers rewards points for buying goods, services, and even visiting the site. FatWallet shares a percentage of its commission with customers as do YouTube and AdWords. Even Chase hands over much of its commission to consumers in exchange for them preferring their Freedom credit cards. Microsoft's Bing tried to emulate this commission-sharing model but decommissioned the program after a few months.

Self-Subsidize Future Commitments Mobile companies have long self-subsidized handsets in exchange for people committing to long-term plans. Financial firms often subsidize new fund expenses to attract investors so they can scale up their assets. Local governments subsidize stadiums or private development in the hopes that the business will generate enough jobs and tax revenues to make up for the expense.

Data Services If your business collects lots of data from transactions, someone will be willing to pay you for it. Before "do not call" lists, your phone number was a hot commodity. Many online services still sell customer data, but it's a fast, tacky way to lose trust. If you are able to aggregate a valuable audience, selling nonpersonally identifiable information or analytics to data or ad companies might be a better route. Even better is controlling the quality and frequency of any third-party offers your customers receive based on their behavioral data.

Free Upgrades with a Purpose

If you surprise a friend with a brand new cell phone but don't pay for service, you're giving them an obligation, not a gift. If, for example, Verizon offered to upgrade any gift cell phone to an Android smartphone, you'd be stoked. Suddenly, your gift looks a lot fancier than that LG flip phone you were going to get. Of course, Verizon requires pricy data plans with all smartphones. That upgrade will now cost much more in monthly charges, possibly losing you a friend in the process.

In 2011, Apple introduced iCloud, a service that allows people to stream music they own to other devices. Apple offered to automatically replace the lower quality tracks with better versions that also have larger file sizes. That might also mean having to buy a higher capacity iPhone or a more expensive data plan. Generally, free storage upgrades could drive more media sales if the same company, in this case Apple, offers both hardware and media.

In the old days, electronic stores that sold CDs or DVDs would throw in one of those players with every TV purchase in hopes of selling media to you in the future. This approach works well with subscriptions and is a digital cousin of the razor and blade model, where you give away the razor and charge for the blades.

Freemium and Upsell

Most software and online services seem to have some kind of basic, free version. The degree of usefulness ranges, depending on how the company makes money. If there are multiple subsidy streams, it can afford to offer more free functionality. Skype offers free calls with video to other Skype subscribers but only makes money if people upgrade. You have to pay to call regular phones, long distance, or have multiple video streams. It remains to be seen how that changes now that Microsoft owns Skype.

The *New York Times* lets readers get 20 free articles a month before locking down the content and asking them to pay. There is a balance in attracting the right kinds of customers this way. Too much functionality creates a base of freeloaders who never pay. Too little means customers feel cheated. This model has a big future as small business growth picks up.

What's better than offering a freemium on one application or service? Creating a marketplace where hundreds of players can do that. Google's updated apps marketplace for small business is particularly well designed. It allows companies to subscribe to tools that do everything from account management to online marketing to collaboration. Its general lack of customer service might hamper the company long term. Others like AppDirect do the same but focus on tools by industry and company size. It's a narrower, more tailored approach that makes it less imposing for most businesses to navigate.

Name Your Price

To this day, I remember having a heated debate about Priceline.com with two friends from work back in 2000. Both insisted that Priceline would be the future of all travel. Everyone would name his or her own price, they argued. I thought that it would have a niche, at best. After all, most people want to know when their vacation starts and what hotel they'll be in. Despite my resounding victory, we managed to stay friends—if only so I could rub it in, here, in book form. Since then, others have employed the name-your-price approach in enough interesting ways that I think it has its place for certain types of services.

There is a New York City cab driver who's been doing this for years. He says he makes much more money than if he used the meter. Guilt is a powerful tool. In 2007, rock band Radiohead parted ways with its record company. The band decided to let people pay whatever they wanted to download its album *In Rainbows*. There were 1.2 million downloads and 38 percent of people paid an average of $6. That's about $2.67 per download or roughly what the band would have received from record company royalties on iTunes and in retail. The Internet is dotted with PayPal tip jars. Leo Laporte's podcast network makes a decent secondary income from monthly or weekly tips. Adam Carolla, who has the top downloaded podcast of all time, asks people to pay him in one of two ways: tell a friend about his show or buy things you'd normally buy on Amazon by clicking through his site. Loyal listeners responded. By mid-2011, Carolla's show was making more than $10,000 a week on Amazon purchase-based tips.

Dynamic Pricing Lessons

I've never shared this with anyone before, but I am a victim of dynamic pricing. Twice in my life I've tried booking a flight online and my browser crashed. When I logged back in, my shopping cart was empty and the price of that same ticket went up by $150. Needless to say, I still hold a grudge. Most people know and accept that airline prices are moving targets. They have dynamic pricing systems that adjust for changes in demand, seasonality, or my vacation plans. Start-up Off & Away is experimenting with selling hotel rooms using prices that adjust based on demand. Overall, I think this will be a big area of opportunity for most high-volume businesses with varying traffic patterns.

Let's use tolls as a proxy for retail traffic. Last year, my dad gave me a ride from Brooklyn to Manhattan. Not only was this a great way to get a life lecture from an all-knowing immigrant while trapped in his car, but it was also a lesson in price inefficiency. Driving is a series of tiny decisions. The biggest one on this trip was whether to take the Brooklyn Bridge (free) or the Battery Tunnel ($5.50 toll). Hundreds of other drivers were making that same choice. Guess which one had unbearable gridlock? Yes, the free one. It was an indicator that the toll was mispriced, at least for that time or for that group of drivers.

After an exhausting, but victorious struggle to convince my dad to pay a toll for the first time, I wondered why tolls don't use the same system as airlines, hotels, and oil companies. By pricing for demand peaks and valleys, municipalities could reduce bottlenecks and improve revenues and safety. Much of this can be a relatively low-tech implementation using existing technologies. No doubt some eager beaver consultants are already on the expressway with decks in hand.

Smarter systems could deliver better pricing. Dynamic pricing should operate at two levels—one based on long, historical trends and the other on intraday patterns. The first step is seeing what patterns look like during different conditions (traffic for tolls or maybe holidays for retailers). Eventually, the long-term data can help discover the right price for any given period, product, or location. Much of that can be done with existing information. In the case of tolls, live traffic data can send price changes, say every 15 minutes, to toll booths. Drivers can receive updates via GPS units, mobile phones, radio, billboards, EZ Pass, or other devices. Newer GPS devices already receive traffic data from satellites, why not toll data? In this scenario, everybody wins. Governments make more money. Drivers save on tolls. And, I reduce my father's lecture time by a whopping 30 percent!

Singapore is piloting a similar system that promises to be extremely low cost. To relieve traffic congestion on its buses, the government will offer people credits for commuting during off-peak hours. Those who accumulate the most points will have a chance to compete for cash in weekly lotteries. Singapore plans to use social tools to help people promote their point balances and winnings in the hopes that the masses overestimate their chances of winning, as people do with other lotteries. Devious.

Retailers and restaurants could use this to clear inventories, get customers to explore new items or categories, or to reprice substitutes for depleted sale items. This approach could also drive off-peak sales at restaurants. Traditional discounts and sales are slow-moving and decision-heavy, but modern technology offers limitless options. You could even apply game mechanics to the shopping experience. The same compulsion that drives addictive online games like Farmville would work for in-store experiences. Overall, prices do not have to increase. In fact, they can be lower as long as some people don't mind donning their bonnets for a 4:00 P.M. dinner.

Long-Term Conditional Pricing

If your goal is to build long-term relationships with customers, conditional pricing is worth exploring. Get people to do something in exchange for a longer or deeper commitment. This kissing cousin of dynamic pricing is especially effective online and in B2B. Most often you see it based on volume—buy 6 get 10 percent off. Amazon uses this tactic for longer term subscription services, offering 15 percent off for automatic reorders of disposable items. Merrill Edge brokerage does this with Bank of America accounts. Merrill dramatically lowers or eliminates trading commissions and fees if you keep a large enough banking balance.

Use Group Leverage to Negotiate Better Rates

The need for unions in the United States is hotly debated in some circles. Some think they've outlived their usefulness since we exited the industrial era. Others believe they protect jobs and give workers needed leverage to negotiate benefits. As more people drift into some hybrid of work and independence, the need for collective bargaining will resurface. And the tools to do it are out there. The first step, in our consumer-driven society, will come from group leverage. I don't mean Groupon or other deals sites. What I envision is people using aggregate buying power to negotiate better rates—in clusters that don't necessarily tie to their employers or communities. It will be based on interest or affinity.

A few businesses are in the early stages of this trend. Dell Swarm in Australia, allows people to place orders for a steeply discounted product they wish to purchase. If enough people commit, Dell will offer that group the chance to buy the item at that price. A Dutch web site, Met de Stroom Mee, lets people negotiate lower energy prices. Once it has 10,000 customers, it will approach energy companies to get lower rates. In India, GrOffr allows people to prebid on real estate. If enough people sign up and the landlord agrees, they can move in, assuming they meet all the usual qualifications. SyncFu is particularly interesting. It lets businesses add group volume discount functionality directly to their sites. Merchants set up the tiers in advance (for example, 10 percent off if they sell 50; 15 percent off for 100, and so on). Site visitors pledge a small down payment with their phones to reserve a spot. When the deal window closes, people get the highest tier discount available. This also creates an incentive for people to actively pester their friends to promote the deal.

These models are just scratching the surface. I can envision manufacturers using this to design future devices with group-demanded features, or, at the very least, to sell custom computer or car configurations. For people or small businesses that are not covered by employer health insurance, ad-hoc consortiums could lead to lower health care or drug costs. The model could also be used for food, travel, or even group recruitment for short-term projects or labor—a sort of virtual corporation.

The End of Money

The final and most pedestrian incentive is good, old-fashioned cash, and it's bittersweet to think that this is the decade in which it will die. Before I explain that statement and what that means to you, I'd like to take you to Russia via Brooklyn, two places and cultures I'm all too familiar with.

Cash Is Czar

Despite my experience in the electronic payments industry, my first love is cash. I'm not necessarily enamored with the accumulation of money (to my dad's disappointment), but with its texture, color, and meaning. As an immigrant, my dad never had or used a credit card. No one I knew ever used one, either. Many of them were too busy splitting the cable signal 12 different ways and complaining about the decline in quality programming. As far as I knew, cash was wealth. And cable was free but unwatchable.

One other term I learned early on was "cash business." For those who didn't grow up in Brooklyn, that means "tax-free." Store owners didn't discourage people from using credit cards, they simply scowled at them until the cards shamefully receded back into their wallets and real money came out. The unstoppable flood of credit card payments must have been tough on those shop owners. The share of income they could hide shrank with every card transaction. It's been years since I lived in the bowels of Brooklyn, but I imagine some things don't change. The one bastion of cash businesses that I know remains is in the old country, Russia. There, you'll see an ad for a $900 a month engineering job, but wonder how anyone could live on that and still have a Mercedes in his garage. Wonder no more. That's only the official wage. The other $3,000 is paid in cold hard cash each month. The company and employee only pay taxes on the official wage and the employee only gets benefits based on that wage. Since both parties are complicit in this scheme, no one has any incentive to report the other's possible indiscretions. The only victims? The tax collector and public services.

Cash Is Dead

While not as cosmically corrupt, this situation is more common in the United States than most realize. In a time of exploding deficits, tax hikes will be unavoidable. Closing the cash loophole is one of the most effective ways to do it. So it's with a twinge of sadness and nostalgia that I declare this decade to be the end of paper money. Don't believe me? It's already begun:

- New York City introduced MetroCards in 1994. When it started offering multiride discounts only on cards, it did not take long for tokens to die. Less than 10 years later, MetroCard was the only game in town. Now, the system is looking to eliminate the middleman. Instead of buying MetroCards, people will be able to pay directly with chip-based phones. As terminals are upgraded and people without bank accounts get a viable alternative card; the MetroCard will be dead over a similar 10-year period.
- Driving tolls have taken the same path. EZ Pass and other compatible systems were introduced in the 1990s, offering discounts, shorter waits at tolls, and the convenience of never having to fish around for quarters between seat cushions. The wireless passes automatically refill from your bank account or credit card whenever the balance runs low.
- By March 2013, the federal government will stop issuing social security checks. The only way recipients can get money is by depositing it in a bank account. The unbanked will get a Direct Express debit card account that will automatically add money to their account and offer one free monthly cash withdrawal. The government will save a billion dollars just on payment processing costs over 10 years.

There is no defensible reason to transport cash. Most employees, for example, already have direct deposit. Maybe I should say all legal employees. In addition to being able to see and tax wages and all spending directly, a cashless system will reduce illegal immigration and force black market payments above ground. (It will also likely attract hackers, but no more than regular currency attracts forgers.) Potentially, that system can also push people to seek substitutes for cash like barter, precious metals, or dog teeth, popularized by Indonesia's Kombai tribe.

The good news is, for most people who are used to using debit and credit cards, not much will change. Even those who use cash extensively will not put up much of a struggle. When New York cab drivers were forced to accept credit cards, the Taxi and Limousine Commission almost had a revolution on its hands. Drivers were upset over processing fees, but I suspect the real fear wasn't over the 3 percent fee, but the 25 percent tax that would be paid by transitioning away from a cash business. The cabbies quickly gave in when they realized cards produced higher tips, and drivers could win expense account business that before only went to car services that accepted corporate cards.

Making the Transition

The two killer apps for cashless payments will be tax collections and incentives. The path to eliminating cash won't lie in forcing change but in seducing people through voluntary actions and incentives the same way Facebook and Android tempt many to surrender privacy for connectivity. For taxes, once all transactions are digital, you won't need an Internal Revenue Service. You'll be able to tax on the fly at rates that can be adjusted by person, product, time, or location. Once money is tracked digitally, sales and income taxes can be made less regressive by automatically charging lower rates to low-wage earners. The end result is simplified tax collection, reporting, and eventually, the complete elimination of tax filing. This system would be a powerful behavior-shaping mechanism as incentives to buy less or more of certain things can be pushed through the system instantaneously. If the city wanted to incentivize shopping in certain remote neighborhoods, it could eliminate taxes for all transactions originated there.

The bulk of the benefit will lie in consumer incentives. Most will gladly give up the right to cash if, like with EZ Pass, they'd get better deals, quicker service, tax or toll discounts, or access to money management tools. These tools could pull in all transaction data that can help budgeting, monitoring, and investing with a single view of all accounts, like a Mint.com on steroids.

The entire transition can be made in less than 10 years if payment networks, banks, mobile companies, and government create a digital payment transition plan with economic incentives for consumers, merchants, and employers to adopt the system.

So What?

At the heart of this IncentiveNation is motivation. My bet in *Econovation* is what motivates people today can and will evolve from the trivial (coupons) to the substantial (building things). As that transition to a maker nation takes hold, businesses need to master the art of human motivation in ways they never have before. They also need to think about motivating and selling to a country of businesses, not one of consumers. This chapter just scratches the surface of what incentives will work in this future America. It's a subject of limitless exploration. Join me at ideafaktory.com for deeper exploration of those possibilities.

CHAPTER

Unfinished Business

We've been through a lot. If you've gotten this far, chances are you recognize the big challenges ahead. You probably also appreciate the big ideas and sense of humor we'll need to face those challenges. Of course, this book was never about reinventing the future; it's about inspiring you to thrive in it. Even the economic predictions in Chapter 3 are not inevitable. They're an opportunity to demand more from government, businesses, and ourselves. That's why I know we have three pieces of unfinished business:

1. Offering a glimpse at the missing half of the Econovation story.
2. Explaining why the very last section of this book is called "Nobody's Bitch" and why it will inspire you.
3. (In the Appendix) providing a peek at how Econovation was made, a summary of all the trends and opportunities, and ways to apply them to your business.

The Missing Link

No matter what those adoring *Econovation* groupies say, this book only tells half a story. After all, I set out to write a business book, not a manifesto. Except for a few diversions here and there, almost every idea in this book is meant to be actionable by a business or individual. Still, that leaves us dealing with the world as it will be, not as it should be. What's missing? Government.

Even in its weak, dysfunctional state, government has the power to correct our economic trajectory. We shouldn't have to worry

189

about default, currency shocks, or Asian bankers repossessing Hawaii. More importantly, the United States has the tools to reclaim the maker mind-set that built this country and made us the envy of the world. It's why my family—and countless others—got on boats, hid under trucks, or floated on inner tubes to get here. A visionary government could, once again, jumpstart that idling engine of possibilities. The book I didn't write (roughly half of my original outline) lays out that vision. It talks about ways to reinvent government—what it should and should not be. That mythical regime embraces our 100-year dash toward automation and our purpose along that path. It creates the kind of incentives and infrastructure that prepare us to compete in a digital future. In that future, the United States needs fewer people but more skilled producers. And government promotes competition, not regulation, to unlock the potential of stagnant industries . . . and stagnant citizens. Like a refugee from a Tony Robbins self-help retreat, that government also works on its biggest character flaw: complexity.

Simplification

I'm not one of those people who thinks we should go back to building our own cabinets and churning our own butter, no matter how delicious that might taste on fresh sourdough. I do think we're off balance. Too many unproductive parts of our economy have flourished, largely with the help of government. Some seem too complex to unwind. Take my word for it, they're not. Whatever you think of the Tea Party movement, after a few drinks even Ralph Nader might admit that it's refreshing to know that people can still form a viable third party that rattles the status quo. Even more rattling—on both sides—wouldn't be a bad thing. We need more competition in politics the same way we need it in business. That conflict will spur better ideas and ultimately, innovation. Otherwise, we'll sit in the same stew, surrounded by stale incumbents and institutions, but expecting fresh, new flavors.

Consider financial regulation and our legal and tax codes. Each is filled with loopholes, big fees, and enough complexity to warrant entire professions built around them. Careers in law, compliance, and tax accounting exist largely because of government policies. I have nothing against accountants. They have perfectly coifed hair, excellent manners, and are almost universally loved by their mothers (who secretly wish they were doctors). But there are 10,000 ways to collect taxes—all of them more efficient than asking 300 million Americans how much they earned last year, then giving them a simple, 800-line form to respond—by mail!

The sum of these huge inefficiencies is a machine that slowly grinds to a halt. I can only imagine what it would take to build the Brooklyn Bridge today. In the late 1800s, the bridge took 13 years to build. It was dangerous work and some died along the way—but we got a f#$(%$' bridge! By comparison, the World Trade Center will take at least 15 years to complete. Yes, the projects and circumstances are different, but we are in the twenty-first century. Lawyers, politicians, and interest groups have increased the complexity of almost everything. A contract that once fit on 2 pages is now 30 and requires countless revisions in between. It's an analog form of encryption. You need a key (lawyer) at each end to encrypt and decrypt what would otherwise be a simple agreement. If there's a second book, I'll explore ways to steer us back to being governed by the spirit of the law, not every excruciating letter of it.

I don't have room here to reinvent government, fix the economy, and help accountants please their mothers. I'll leave that for another time and place. What it comes down to is a choice. In one hand, there's a society mired in filling out tax forms, suing each other for every tiny injustice, and making each step toward progress long and arduous. In the other hand is a collective of smart, enterprising patriots building the next Google, a faster aircraft, or just a humble cabinet. Which is it going to be?

Nobody's Bitch

I bet you didn't expect *that* to be the subtitle of my inspirational conclusion. The more I thought about it, the more I realized this book isn't really about economic innovation at all. It's about emancipation. But emancipation from what? A new form of slavery has slowly crept into our lives. Its danger lies in how subtle, subversive, and seductive it is.

Subjugation Cake

We've baked quite a layer cake of subjugation (see Figure 9.1).

Figure 9.1   Subjugation Cake

At a macro level, the United States surrendered its engine of growth and production to China, which doesn't wake up each morning thinking, "how can I make a portly American happy today?". That didn't seem to bother us. Government and citizen alike racked up debt buying everything in sight, only to be left with that empty, uncomfortable feeling of owing someone money. In the process, large corporations and wealthy citizens successfully negotiated tax rates down to virtually nothing. Only about 9 percent of government revenues come from corporate taxes. Those same companies, with the help of charismatic lobbyists bearing delicious steak dinners, convinced politicians to allow productive jobs to pour out of our economy. What remained were administrative, stagnant jobs with waning salaries and few opportunities for personal satisfaction. Some dared to start ventures, but too few to close America's yawning growth gap. Many creative, ambitious people didn't even dare to try. They were paralyzed by fear of failure, lack of know-how, or limited access to financing. Or, they faced the very real problem of paying off college debt, providing health coverage for their families, or paying for their kids' education. So they remained—chained to their desks, toiling away in hollow obscurity—and did not start businesses that would grow the economy and enrich their lives.

As China, India, and Brazil took slices of cake off the table, the vast majority of Americans remained mesmerized by gadgets, games, and coupons. Is that all we are? Shoppers? Smart, capable people spending their days chasing deals, signing up for discounts, and promoting them to friends on Facebook. Is that what this is all about? Really?

It doesn't have to stay that way.

Prison Break

Now would be a good time to delete that Shopify app from your iPhone and install the Nobody's Bitch app. It doesn't run on a phone. It doesn't need batteries. And, it offers no discounts. It only has only one function—unlocking your passion.

I wrote a lot about makers and the maker mentality. Now is the time for it to come to fruition. In the coming decade, you'll either witness or lead that change. There are more tools than ever to take you in either direction—consumer or producer. You decide. Technology and social media are tools that can keep you bedridden for days playing World of Warcraft, or they can help you crowdfund a new business. If you choose the maker path, not only will a world of possibilities open up, you'll have more support than you realize. Everyone from family to friends to government will work harder than you think to get you the cash and connections to help you succeed. You'll also find plenty of other, passionate makers doing the same, forming communities to help each other along the way.

Whatever you decide, it should start with passion. Even if it means working for free at the beginning. If you're good, the money will follow. My hope is that you don't fall back on the easy thing. Building a web site is easy; anyone can do it. I would never discourage it, but I'd love for more people to choose the road less traveled. Economic growth will come from the big-ticket items that foreigners will buy in droves. And you're not that far from making anything you can dream up. Companies like Ponoco and Quirky will help you design and build that dream power adapter, birdhouse, or automatic kiwi peeler.

I know not everyone is looking to start a business. Many will continue working for large corporations or government institutions. But they too have a deeper purpose—to buy from and invest in the next generation of American makers and risk-takers. Not every risk-taker will seek profit. Some will prefer to start charities or foundations. I have friends who have done just that, and I admire and respect them greatly (I mean you, Amy!). If you're on the fence, please allow me to sway you toward profit. I've thought a lot about what is truly charitable and sustainable. My conclusion: A successful, growing business is the ultimate charity. If the world only had charities, all of Sally Struthers' kids would starve. There would be no companies or salaries to sponsor that cup of coffee a day you're not buying. Generate many salaries and you empower a new generation of givers.

If I could inspire just one thing with this little pep talk, it's this: I hope the thing you do right after you finish this book is put on some Barry White and get busy. That's right, I want you to procreate, even at the risk of damaging these precious pages. Why? You obviously get it. You appreciate great literature, go to great lengths to find new ideas, and you can probably afford college tuition. We need more people just like you. Whether you have kids or not, I'd like you to have more. When you do, I hope that you teach them to solder. As you raise this next generation of makers, my dream is that you teach them to embrace imperfection, change tires, and build tree houses. If your daughter doesn't own a hacksaw by the age of seven, I'll feel like a failure. Moreover, I hope you teach her to sell . . . or lend her to a Mormon family who'll do it for you.

I know creating something isn't easy. I've struggled with my own duality. On one side, there's a fearless, defiant innovator. On the other, the son of immigrant parents who instilled a fear of everything in him—except working for someone else. I'm starting to come around and overcome those fears. I hope you do, too. An unsuccessful business is not the biggest risk you face. You can forgive yourself for failing, but you'll always regret not trying.

Feeling empowered? Good. Now, go do it.

P.S. I know you'll still go out and buy things. When you do, try to do it at a small business. Get to know the person selling those things. Do you trust him? Could that relationship be more satisfying than the 10 percent coupon at that Megamart? Maybe someday, that item you buy will be made *here* by someone you know—or maybe even by you.

Applying Econovation

How the Sausage Was Made

This chapter is a summary of the key trends and a little behind-the-scenes look at the process behind *Econovation*. They say, never ask how the sausages were made . . . you've been warned.

Approach

Over the past decade of leading innovation, I saw a lot of patterns, and sadly, PowerPoints. I've distilled the four elements essential for innovating at scale. I call this process the 4Cs of Innovation™. There are a lot of details beneath each element, but at a high level, they are: Context, Creativity, Capabilities, and Culture. (See Figure A.1.)

The focus of the first three chapters in *Econovation* is on the macroeconomic part of Context (Figure A.2). The rest of *Econovation* explores the second C, Creativity, and the specific opportunities that will thrive in light of our economic conditions.

Hindsight to Foresight

It's easy enough to Econovate in hindsight. When I wrote about innovations during the Great Depression, it seemed obvious why supermarkets would succeed in an era of expensive gas and fragmented shops. My approach looked something like Figure A.3. The opportunity themes came last.

A lot has changed since the Great Depression. We are knee-deep in clues to our economic future. The conditions that made Twinkies a success in the 1930s, or HMOs possible in the 1970s have changed. Constraints and incentives are evolving. The government subsidizes corn syrup but scorns salt. It incentivizes building Wal-Marts and props up naughty banks. Every day is Christmas for somebody and Lent for someone else. The flows of capital and power are moving

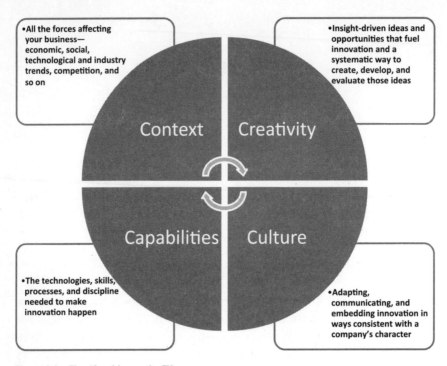

Figure A.1   The 4Cs of Innovation™

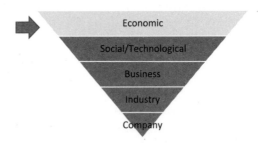

Figure A.2   Context—Trends Affecting Innovation

Figure A.3   Hindsight—Evaluating Depression Era Innovation

Figure A.4   Foresight—Econovation

from west to east, from consumers to corporations, from shag rugs to red carpets. Most importantly, the world is becoming more complex. There is more of everything: cereals in aisle six, ways to buy stocks, tools to call Mom, sources for coupons, and IT guys named Rajeev.

So, for *Econovation,* I had to take a different approach. As you can see in Figure A.4, I started with clues from our past and present to project likely economic conditions. Some interesting opportunity themes started to emerge. From those, I researched and brainstormed (mostly by myself—a lonely and thankless exercise!) to come up with a list of possible innovations that would thrive in this future economy.

All Together Now

Figure A.5 shows how economic trends will impact U.S. businesses. Some create downward pressure on inputs, while others, like innovation, stimulation, and a weak dollar, help exports. (These are just the mechanics—all the content is in the book's prior chapters).

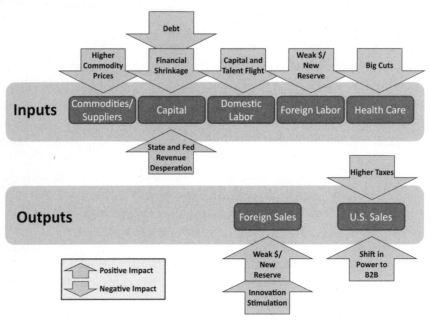

Figure A.5   Econovation in Practice

To make your life a little easier, in Tables A.1 and A.2, I mapped most of the big ideas from the book according to which business inputs (supply, capital, domestic labor, foreign labor, and health care) and outputs (domestic sales, foreign sales) they'll impact.

Table A.1   Opportunity Summary: Inputs

	Commodities/ Suppliers	Capital	Domestic Labor	Foreign Labor	Health Care
Sell Actualiz-ation			• Free labor • Tiny project, tiny pay • Social identity as leverage		
Capital Magnet	• Barter • Hedging • Energy tech • Print the future	• Barter • Shared infrastructure • Lock in capital advantage • Hedging	• Reverse outsourcing	• Reverse outsourcing	• Remote health care
Make Makers		• Alternative financing	• College in two • Teach creativity • Align with demand • Rate schools • Alternative financing • Vocational training and apprenticeships		
Liberate Micropreneurs		• Crowdfunding + alternative capital models • New incubators • Surplus real estate	• Entrepreneurship and education • New incubators	• Surplus real estate	• Health care as investment
Incentive-Nation	• Group leverage • Kill cash	• Kill cash	• Hire psychologists • Incentivize obsolescence		• Behavioral bribery

Table A.2   Opportunity Summary: Outputs

	Foreign Sales	U.S. Sales
Sell Actualization		• Producer identity • Secure future
Capital Magnet	• Sell to BRICs • Shared infrastructure • Hedging • Disneyfication/bundling • Print the future • Energy tech	• Here commerce • Localism • Barter • Hedging • Remote health care
Make Makers	• Automation	• Automation • Kindergarten shop class
Liberate Micropreneurs	• Micro-Disneyfication • Build ecosystems	
Incentive-Nation	• Kill cash	• Micro-incentives • Elasticity • Behavioral bribery • New pricing and incentive models • Kill cash

About the Author

Steve Faktor is the former vice president of growth and innovation at American Express, where he developed and incubated numerous growth ventures including Zync, LoyaltyEdge, and Private Sales, a joint venture with Vente Privee. In his career, Steve has created several $100-million-plus businesses, managed American Express' Chairman's Innovation Fund, and deployed three enterprise-level innovation programs. Steve is the founder of Blue Beacon Partners, LLC, which helps start-ups and corporations innovate new products and services, think big, and build a sustainable growth pipeline. Previously, Steve was a senior innovation and strategy executive at Citibank and MasterCard. As a management consultant at Arthur Andersen, Steve led strategy, marketing, and technology projects for clients like WPP Group (Ogilvy), Samsung, JVC, Bombardier, Boise Cascade, Omnicom Group, and PSEG.

As a futurist, innovator, and digital payments expert, Steve is a popular global keynote speaker on future growth opportunities. Steve also leads innovation workshops, ideation, and training sessions based on his proprietary 4Cs of Innovation™ methodology. An author with a satirical touch, his latest musings on trends in business can be read at ideafaktory.com.

Steve has a BS in Economics and Accounting from Stern School of Business at New York University. He lives in New York City and is actively involved in Junior Achievement, writing, travel, emerging technology, and the arts.

Index